A PHILOSOPHY

A Philosophy of Pessimism

Stuart Sim

REAKTION BOOKS

Dedicated to the memory of my late sister,
Fiona Cargill Sim (1947–2013)

Published by
Reaktion Books Ltd
33 Great Sutton Street
London EC1V 0DX, UK

www.reaktionbooks.co.uk

First published 2015

Copyright © Stuart Sim 2015

Printed and bound in Great Britain
by Bell & Bain, Glasgow

A catalogue record for this book is available from the British Library

ISBN 978 1 78023 505 9

Contents

Preface

Ian Dury once had a hit song entitled 'Reasons To Be Cheerful' (1979), which was a fairly jaunty, upbeat number; but this book is about the reasons *not* to be cheerful. Reasons, in fact, to be pessimistic about the human condition in general. There is no shortage of these. We can find them not just in the modern world around us, although they are numerous enough there, but throughout world history in the work of philosophers, theologians, writers, composers, thinkers and creative artists of all types. We have to wonder why pessimism has proved to have such an enduring hold over the ages, exercising so many minds, and why it seems just as relevant to us in the twenty-first century as it was in the past, despite all the undeniable improvements in the quality of life that the modern world has brought us. Why should we be pessimistic now?

Surveying its historical legacy enables us to recognize that pessimism is not just a symptom of our current cultural woes. Nor is it an abnormal state (as your friends may well keep hinting to you if you are that way inclined). Instead, it is of long standing and eminently defensible as a worldview. Furthermore, pessimism is not a message of doom and gloom but a very considered response to human nature and its full range of traits. There really are reasons not to be cheerful – good ones – and it is to our advantage to know what these are. Even if you think of yourself as an essentially optimistic kind of person, disposed to look on the bright side of life, this knowledge should give you cause to reconsider your outlook and appreciate the virtue of twenty-first-century pessimism.

ONE

The Glass is Always Half-full?
Countering the Optimists

There are many reasons to despair at the state of the world today: climate change and global warming; widespread 'humanitarian disasters' due to war, famine and political corruption; religious intolerance and the growing influence of fundamentalist belief; political terrorism; racism; discrimination against ethnic minorities; sexism; the list could go on and on. Reflect on such phenomena at any length and it can be very difficult indeed not to become deeply pessimistic about human existence. I am one of those who do reflect, a committed pessimist, if you like, and my aim is to convince you not only that it makes sense to adopt a pessimistic attitude towards life, the universe and everything, but that we should regard pessimism as a positive condition. All of us probably swing from pessimism to optimism and back again in the daily round, but there is a very good case to be put for gravitating towards the former position in your general outlook.

If the notion of a 'positive pessimism' sounds paradoxical, a persuasive defence can be mounted for it. Once we appreciate that there is a seam of pessimism running through our history, and that there have always been good reasons for cultivating such an outlook, we will be in a better position to understand how we can now turn it to positive account.

Philosophers, theologians, authors, creative artists in general, even scientists, have collectively contributed to a discourse of pessimism, and they have found a ready audience for their message across all cultures. They have insisted that we face up to the more desperate aspects of the human condition – and there are quite a few of these to ponder. How that discourse of pessimism has developed and its multi-faceted nature – and, more importantly, what we can learn from it – is my subject. I intend to explore the arguments for pessimism as a justifiable basis for a lifestyle, and consider why assuming that the glass is always half-empty could be of more benefit to humanity than a blinkered optimism that everything will eventually turn out all right as long as we keep faith. Even the most casual glance at human history will suggest that, on the contrary, things all too often turn out wrong – sometimes horribly wrong. It seems only sensible, therefore, to cultivate a mindset that is prepared for bad outcomes to continue to be a significant part of the human experience. We need to keep the dark side of human affairs at the forefront of our consciousness, to counter the optimists and their rosy outlook. Perhaps, after all, it is more rational to adopt an essentially pessimistic attitude towards our collective lot: to 'wake up to reality and be a pessimist'.

The word 'pessimism' itself is derived from the Latin *pessimus*, meaning 'worst', and came into usage in the late eighteenth century; 'optimism' comes from *optimus*, the Latin for 'best'. Most current dictionary definitions of pessimism emphasize that sense of seeing the worst aspects of situations as the most likely to occur, and the working definition for this particular project will be built from that point.

It is important to note that pessimism is to be differentiated not just from optimism but also from fatalism. Pessimism involves a striving against the odds, even when you believe these are overwhelmingly stacked against you and that the worst outcome almost inevitably looms (the 'almost' being crucial). Fatalism is more in the nature of surrendering to events that we are powerless to change. The latter is an attitude widely attributed in Western culture, rightly or wrongly, to

Islamic belief. Pessimism and optimism are not necessarily mutually exclusive positions, however: pessimists can be optimistic about some things, optimists pessimistic about others in their turn. All of us are capable of the kind of mood swings in response to changing circumstances that can generate feelings of either condition at any given point in our lives, even though we might feel that we are largely disposed towards one side rather than the other. Optimists can be knocked back by severe ill health, for example, and pessimists inwardly hope to be given a clean bill of health when they visit their doctor with suspicious symptoms. It is perfectly natural to have experience of both pessimism and optimism in your own life, and this is by no means designed to be an argument that it is best to remain firmly stuck in the former state for your every waking moment.

Yet even if there is a spectrum of possible responses in any individual's life that we oscillate between, what soon becomes apparent is that each outlook has certain recurrent features that seem to point predominantly in one direction rather than the other, and that these will eventually assert themselves in attitudes and behaviour. It rarely takes long to distinguish a pessimist from an optimist, and it is the general attitude each sustains, rather than particular instances that could be interpreted either way, that will be the focus of this book. The case to be put is that pessimism should become a dominant factor in your worldview because it is a trait worth developing.

As to what it means to be a pessimist, a key feature is that the pessimist does not give in: he or she may well believe that their actions are likely to fail, even that the balance of probability is always strongly inclined in that direction, but that does not cause that individual to withdraw from the world – or, ultimately, to lose hope entirely. That is the state of mind of the mythological figure of Sisyphus as he endlessly pushes a boulder uphill, an image that to the French existentialist author Albert Camus pretty much summed up the human condition. You might say that for pessimists hope does indeed spring eternal, although rarely justifiably, and that they are always somewhat surprised if justification ever does prove to be forthcoming. As a native Scot I am decidedly pessimistic about the prospects for the Scottish international football team on the basis of past experience, but that does not mean that I give up supporting them whenever they play with the unspoken hope (no matter how residual) that this time around things will turn out differently.

Optimists, on the other hand, do not find successful outcomes at all surprising. Rather, they expect them: failures are regarded as very much the exception, not the rule, and do not shake their generally sanguine outlook on life and human nature. They persist in what the philosopher Roger Scruton has called the '"best case" fallacy', assuming that the best case will always apply.[1] Scruton's pessimism is based on a far less forgiving vision of social and political history, in which he notes how often the best case fails to transpire (although I do not at all share the reactionary conclusions that he draws from this). Just take note of how often the excuse of 'human error' is offered up when something goes badly wrong, as if that explained the event away satisfactorily and allowed us to carry on much as before. It should make us more worried for the future, because human error is simply part of the landscape and is highly unlikely ever to be eradicated. And human errors when it comes to things like nuclear power stations can, as we know, have truly dire consequences.

Pessimists tend to be far more aware of the dark side of human nature, and are unconvinced that this has been declining in significance throughout human history, particularly in our 'enlightened' modern era, with its emphasis on the power of reason: even reason cannot really explain away human error. The latter period, with its litany of massively destructive wars, savage purges and large-scale ethnic cleansing episodes, does not dispose the pessimist to put much faith in the innate sense of goodness and compassion in human nature; not when the 'best case' so frequently lets us down. Neither does the growth of organized crime into a political and economic global powerhouse, as in the case of 'narco' states such as Mexico, with ruthless drug cartels controlling large swathes of its territory, prove any more inspiring. The dark side is still very much with us, and pessimists refuse to turn a blind eye to this in the way that optimists are only too prone to do.

We might wonder if we can equate pessimism with depression. Pessimists can certainly become quite depressed when thinking about the apparently eternal return of humanity's dark side, but the more acute the depressive condition, the more disabling it becomes and the closer it approaches outright fatalism. In particularly severe cases, depressives simply give up trying to cope. It is worth pointing out, too, that depression is a recognized medical condition, whereas pessimism is more in the nature of a personality trait – and, I am going to argue, an eminently defensible trait at that. There is a saying among hospital doctors, whose work, especially at junior level, can involve long and antisocial hours, that has an appropriately pessimistic ring to it in line with the definition offered here: 'Life's a bitch, then you're on call.' Precisely: life may well be a bitch, but you just grit your teeth and turn up for your all-night on-call duties regardless (said with considerable sympathy as the husband of a hospital doctor).

One connection I do want to make, however, is between pessimism and scepticism. Scepticism is a long-running and well-established, if still controversial, tradition in Western philosophy, and it can be interpreted as encouraging pessimism since it promotes an attitude of doubt (often extreme doubt) about what we can ever know with any certainty. We may think we have foolproof knowledge of the world, but to sceptics this is merely an illusion: absolute proof is never available to us, and never will be. In other words, we have only beliefs of a greater or lesser strength or convincing-ness – and of course, such beliefs will vary across the whole population. Pushed far enough, this seems to entail that we can never really make sense of our world.

Opponents tend to argue that scepticism is a highly pessimistic form of theory, and that it leads away from cooperation among individuals, rendering action to bring about change (in politics, say) as fairly pointless. How could we ever agree on action if there is no certain knowledge to build upon? Theories like existentialism, which posit a world without any transcendental meaning that would give a sense of purpose to our lives, tax philosophers and creative artists alike in trying to find reasons not to be pessimistic about the human condition. I should point out that it is scepticism in its philosophical sense that I will be referring to throughout the book. 'Scepticism' is a term that is often used very loosely these days, as in the case of Euroscepticism or global warming scepticism, whose followers have no doubt at all about their own beliefs but simply deny that their opponents have any valid argument or credible evidence to put forward. The term 'denialism' has been coined to describe these attitudes, and is much more appropriate than 'scepticism'. To the philosophical sceptic, denialism is based on the hidden premise of the right-ness of one's position, and since such a premise is never justifiable it cannot qualify as proper scepticism. I intend to be a proper sceptic.

* * *

Optimists and pessimists have been in a long-running dia-logue, and it is worth considering a contemporary work that takes pessimists to task: Matt Ridley's *The Rational Optimist: How Prosperity Evolves*. Ridley's argument is that pessimists are people who refuse to acknowledge the progress that humankind has made over the centuries, especially in the modern era, with all its technological advances and general improvements in the standard of living. I do have a personal angle in picking out Ridley as my representative optimist: I have shared a stage with him at a book festival, where I objected that places in the developing world like Haiti did not seem to have experienced much in the way of improvement in their living standards, only for Ridley to respond that it was their own fault that Western companies were not investing there, because their planning laws were so restrictive. That is one way of explaining away developing world poverty, I suppose, but not one I find at all convincing. Nor do I subscribe to his idea that all it requires to alleviate developing world poverty is to increase Western investment and further the cause of globalization: we are on completely different political wavelengths there.

For Ridley, not to be uncompromisingly optimistic about our prospects for the future is to be almost wilfully contrary: optimism is the only rational response he can imagine given the evidence he can produce. We have more of everything than ever before, and far greater control over the environment to ensure that this trend continues. Hence the resounding sentiments with which Ridley closes *The Rational Optimist*: 'The twenty-first century will be a magnificent time to be alive. Dare to be an optimist.'[2] We can only assume that Haitian politicians just have not been 'daring' enough to join the brave new world that optimists are so generously offering.

But no, I do not think we should take up Ridley's 'dare'. He may be right to argue that there are many things for which we should be grateful, but being grateful is surely not quite the same thing as being optimistic. We should all be grateful that the standard of healthcare has so radically improved in modern times; although if you live in America, and are not a rich citizen, you might well be extremely pessimistic about how much of that you will ever be able to access, given the country's notoriously profit-greedy private medical schemes. I take it to be the role of the pessimist to keep raising such awkward examples. Ridley has a rather dismissive attitude towards our 'unenlightened' pre-modern past, however, and an apparently boundless faith that progress – in his sense of the term – can continue indefinitely. In that sense, his book becomes an instructive case study of card-carrying optimism in full-blown action. Things can only get better for this author.

According to Ridley, we should be optimistic about humanity's future given the huge strides we have made in overcoming so many of the problems that beset the lives of even our very recent ancestors. It is up to the pessimist, however, to object that this is an incorrigibly Western-centric viewpoint; the developing world is another case altogether, with modernity still barely impinging on the lives of many. Ridley bases his claim on a particular view of the past, which was not just another country, but a rather sad and benighted one with a lifestyle that we should be heartily glad we no longer have to experience. Nostalgia for past times is simply misplaced, an instance of refusing to face up to the facts. Do you yearn for the 'simplicity, tranquility, sociability and spirituality [of] life in the distant past'?[3] Well, just remember that if you had not died young from any of the numerous infectious diseases so prevalent in earlier days, the average life expectancy in England in 1800 was merely 40. Time to give up your romantic visions, and to cease complaining about the unequal distribution of money and resources around the globe, because in the long term everyone benefits: 'The rich have got richer, but the poor have done even better.'[4] It is a sentiment that you can hear being repeated regularly by neoliberal economic theorists, as will be discussed in more detail in chapter Three; the 'trickle-down effect', as it is called. Such evidence is enough to convince them, and Ridley, of the rightness of the free-market system that has developed in the last couple of centuries. To express any reservations about this is to give into a misguided pessimism.

Ridley is merely the tip of the iceberg, however, and once you start exploring the record you will find that optimists have much to answer for in the contemporary world. Excessive optimism has led to far more problems than pessimism ever has. Just consider the sociologist Zygmunt Bauman's words about what happened when Soviet optimism, in the early years of that regime, decided to re-engineer nature by means of a series of 'grand designs', so that it could be made to serve their planning specifications:

> Deserts were irrigated (but they turned into salinated bogs); marshlands were dried (but they turned into deserts); massive gas-pipes criss-crossed the land to remedy nature's whims in distributing its resources (but they kept exploding with a force unequalled by the natural disasters of yore) . . . Raped and crippled, nature failed to deliver the riches one hoped it would; the total scale of design only made the devastation total.[5]

Optimism backfired badly in these instances, and it is worth remembering them when weighing up some of the more recent schemes to overcome 'nature's whims' and force it 'to deliver' its hidden 'riches' up to us. We might reflect on what has happened to the Aral Sea, for example, which has now shrunk to a mere fraction of its original size due to just such a scheme where rivers were diverted, all but wiping out what was once a thriving fishing industry which was economically vital to the local population.

Fracking is worth citing in this context, too. So are any of the schemes to extract oil from under the seabed in remote areas, as in the major oil companies' plans to drill under the Arctic Ocean for its as-yet untapped reserves. The latter is something that global warming will make easier by melting the sea ice cover: the irony could not be heavier. Fears that fracking might cause earthquakes, which some scientists have warned could well occur depending on a region's particular geological conditions, are simply dismissed by the corporate giants pushing for the practice; after all, they stand to make a great deal of profit by exploiting the world's insatiable appetite for energy to keep its economy growing. But if they prove to be wrong in the way that the Soviet authorities so plainly were, what then? Optimists are quite happy to take risks on such projects, barely conceding them to be such; daring can all too easily shade into blind trust, and politicians are only too capable of being led down that route. Pessimists, at the very least, weigh those risks up carefully, and are prepared to turn them down if the levels of doubt and uncertainty seem too prohibitive. Pessimists do not generally seek out risk, although they will face up to it if circumstances absolutely demand it.

Then there is the phenomenon of climate change, already having a marked impact in places like the Arctic, where the ice cover is retreating even more rapidly than scientists had predicted it would in the mid-2010s. Greenland now even has a 'lake district' where once was there was a year-round ice sheet. The knock-on effect of rising average temperatures on sea levels could be really dramatic, leading to widespread coastal flooding across the globe that could make many of the world's major cities all but uninhabitable: New York and London, for example, as well as most of the heavily populated Eastern seaboard of the USA, which would create severe problems for the world economy. Even if this is a topic which is susceptible to doom-mongering, which can easily encourage fatalism, it should still give us pause for thought. Are the oil companies, and the denialists in their wake, falling prey to the best-case fallacy?

Low-lying countries like Bangladesh are feeling the effects of rising sea levels even now, with regular flooding creating havoc in many of its delta communities. Several Pacific islands are fast disappearing beneath the ocean: the island states of Kiribati and Tuvalu are predicted to become largely uninhabitable in the near future and are already debating possible evacuation plans for their citizens. Yet global warming deniers refuse to acknowledge such evidence ('Gaia's revenge' to such commentators as the environmental campaigner James Lovelock[6]), exhorting us instead to be optimistic about the likely changes longer term, which they claim will be insignificant in their effect as far as most of us are concerned. That is, if they happen at all – as many deniers vehemently question.

Not surprisingly, the denialists tend to adopt a gung-ho attitude towards fracking and Arctic Ocean oil exploration, effectively accusing objectors of a lack of daring. Pessimists and sceptics would be minded to recommend caution instead, on the basis of where so many daring grand designs have led in the past. Optimism really does have its perils, and we should be alerted to these. Joshua Foa Dienstag has claimed that 'pessimism is a philosophical technique from which political practices can be derived.'[7] To oppose optimism with a positive pessimism in situations like the above is inevitably to articulate a political position, and I am entirely happy to do so.

The grand designs being put forward by science as ways of dealing with ongoing global warming hardly put the pessimist's mind at rest, or quell the sceptic's doubts, either. To be fair to the scientific profession, they regard these as very much a last resort to cope with the public's resistance to significant changes in its lifestyle in the meantime (especially in energy use). Among the solutions mooted for restricting temperature rises are: placing white sheeting over large areas of the planet's major deserts, such as the Sahara and the Gobi, to reflect sunlight back out into space; painting whole cities white to achieve the same effect (particularly in the hottest parts of the globe); stationing chains of giant mirrors, 55,000 of them in one estimate, out in deep space to prevent a significant amount of sunlight ever reaching the Earth in the first place; replanting vast tracts of the globe's surface with forests to absorb more carbon; and dumping a massive amount of iron in the Southern Ocean to increase the growth of carbon-absorbing algae there.[8] The more worrying the reports become from organizations studying global warming, such as the IPCC (International Panel on Climate Change), the wilder and less practical the schemes put forward to counteract the process become too.

All such geoengineering schemes represent acts of faith, because they cannot be guaranteed to have the desired effect: they could, in fact, have the opposite effect to the one intended. Yet if we were to reach the tipping point that necessitated their introduction (Amazon logging being the kind of practice that could push us over the line), then you can bet the optimists would be loud in their support: trust to human ingenuity and all that. Even the less grandiose schemes that have been tried so far to develop green energy to replace our reliance on fossil fuel, and thus reduce the current level of carbon emissions, have had mixed success at best. Often these are even counter-productive. Turning agricultural land over to plants that can be used to manufacture biofuel (ethanol), for instance, has cut down that available for food production. Farmers in the American Midwest, formerly one of the world's largest sources of wheat, have discovered that they can make more profit by shifting to biofuel production, and many have done just that; good for them, perhaps, but not for those at the other end of the food chain. A similar pattern is noticeable elsewhere, creating shortages in basic food crops. This has driven prices up on the global market, which has been particularly hard on poorer countries, who spend a larger proportion of their national assets on staple food commodities than the West does.

It is also worth pointing out that all such schemes are designed to enable us to sustain a growth-based economy that will keep delivering the improvements to our lifestyle that optimists like Ridley are praising so enthusiastically, as if it were our true destiny as a species: *Homo economicus* as the high point of evolution. For all the efforts of the greens and the de-growth advocates, we are still collectively fixated on that objective, and it suits the corporate sector only too well to go on complying with what it entails: 'growthism', as it is coming to be known. Profit has a distinct tendency to trump social conscience most of the time, and I find it very difficult not to be pessimistic about what this says about our culture. All too often it brings to the fore one of humanity's least attractive traits: greed.[9]

Yet despite such glaring examples as those outlined above, optimism continues to thrive and can be found where you might least expect it. Another recent book even contrives to be optimistic about the effects of war; the historian Ian Morris argues that the massive loss of life in the various wars of the twentieth century was counteracted by the population gains made elsewhere in the world in the same period. War gives rise to technological benefits for us all, and is a key factor in driving up living standards. This is, of course, seen to be an unqualified 'good', even if it does involve some collateral damage on the way there: 'the larger societies created by war have also – again, over the long term – made us richer.'[10] We can only conclude that optimism is very much in the eye of the beholder: war may make economic sense, but surely not emotional sense. It would be a sad comment on humankind if we had to depend on war to drive forward technological progress (which invariably drives up corporate profit too, of course). Even Morris expresses a similar sentiment in the early stages of his book, but thinks we just have to accept that this is so, that being the lesson that history teaches us. For those of us of a pessimistic bent, however, history has many other lessons to teach us than that, and I shall be identifying as many as I can throughout the remainder of this book.

* ✻ *

Pessimism can, and should, be regarded as a more realistic attitude to adopt towards the human condition than a blinkered optimism of the kind to be noted nowadays in neo-liberal ideology, as well as much evangelical religion – as long as you are one of the 'chosen' few to benefit, that is. If you are outside the charmed circle of such true believers, however, you need to be very much on your guard for the appearance of worst-case scenarios: they can happen, they do happen and there is no point in pretending otherwise. Life can indeed be a bitch, but it is all we have to work with. Interestingly enough, there is some recent research claiming that hope can make your life more miserable, and that people who give this up can find themselves becoming happier and more at ease with their situation. In an article in the *Economic Journal*, the authors of a German survey on the unemployed found that this group of individuals became happier when they retired. They no longer had to convince themselves to be optimistic about their prospects, despite the fact that they had not materially improved on retirement.[11] While this may not be an argument for pessimism as such, it is certainly one against undue optimism.

It is often pointed out that although pessimists may well be right much of the time, they do not have as much fun as optimists, so why not choose to be an optimist instead? There can be some truth in that, but it does depend very much on how you interpret pessimism, and how strategic you are in its use. There are times when it self-evidently is not a good idea to have fun: in the middle of a natural disaster or a war zone, for example, or when climate change is making your habitat unliveable. That encourages the kind of seriousness that pessimists feel we should be exhibiting much more of in our lives. Black humour can surface on such occasions, but that is different – and quite compatible with a pessimistic outlook. Perhaps pessimism can be carried too far on occasion, but I am concentrating on what it means in terms of a worldview which is taking into account the dark side of human nature and keeping in mind our well-documented fallibility as a species. Being aware that the 'worst' can and does happen, and more often than is comfortable for our security, is an unavoidable reaction that strengthens the more we reflect on the historical record.

TWO

The 'Doomsday Clock' is Always with Us: Pessimism in History

Pessimism about humanity's prospects has been expressed at pretty well every point in recorded history, whether those prospects have been held to derive from our own actions or from circumstances outside our control – and, if the former, whether our actions have been taken to be the product of nature or nurture. Religion has been a particularly fertile ground for the development of pessimism, as, latterly, has science, with both making us very aware of what lies beyond the power of our actions. Where once it was the immutability of the divine will that gave cause for grave concern, now it is phenomena such as climate change and the possible collapse of the environment around us. Neither give much scope for optimism. The *Bulletin of the Atomic Scientists* has devised what it calls the 'Doomsday Clock' to report on the threat that technological developments pose to human-kind. The cover of its May 2014 issue announces that, thanks to our present state of technological 'progress' and its increas-ingly evident destructive impact on the environment, 'It is 5 minutes to midnight.' Whether or not we could, or should, arrest this process (there is strident opposition to the findings by a vocal lobby of climate-change deniers) is a topic of con-siderable public debate at present. There is no shortage of reasons why the pessimistic temperament has persisted through the ages and why so many have been so exercised by their culture's current version of the 'doomsday clock' ticking down.

* ✳ *

The question of one's salvation looms large in Christianity, and nowhere more so than in Protestantism, which emphasized this doctrine to a far greater extent than the tradition of Catholicism it had broken away from in the Reformation. Protestantism encouraged a sense of individualism (it is easy to forget how modern a concept individualism is) that had far-reaching implications in both religious and political terms. Under Protestantism individuals were required to take more personal responsibility for the state of their individual souls, and in some branches of Protestantism this could be taken to quite extreme lengths. This had much to do with belief in the concept of predestination, which, while having relevance to Christians of any persuasion – it is derived from certain passages of the Bible, and therefore open to interpretation by any believer – became particularly strong among certain Protestant sects. Those most influenced by the theology of the sixteenth-century French reformer Jean Calvin were at the forefront of this trend.

Calvinism was particularly influential on the Continent (in Switzerland and the Netherlands, for example), but it also made substantial inroads in Britain. Calvinist theology had a notable impact in Scotland, with Scots Presbyterianism developing along those lines, and also in the early days of Anglicanism in England. There was a recognizably Calvinist movement within the Anglican Church in the late sixteenth and early seventeenth centuries, and although a more moderate tendency was to prevail (and has largely done so since), the theology subsequently proved to be very congenial to the growing sectarian movement that developed over the course of the seventeenth century. Groups like the Baptists, for example, incorporated many of Calvin's doctrines into their worldview.

Calvinist theology poses the interesting dilemma of how we could ever be held responsible for our actions if God had decided our ultimate spiritual fate before we were even born.

This is what the theory of predestination lays down, with no exceptions to the rule; the only doubt among Calvinists concerns whether God made this decision before or after the fall of humankind, with schools of thought on both views ('prelapsarian' and 'postlapsarian' respectively). Taking this into even more problematical territory, however, is the insistence that the individual is nevertheless to blame for his or her own state of damnation (or reprobation, in theological parlance). Equally problematical is the principle that individuals cannot take any credit for their own salvation either (election, as it was known), because that is purely the result of God's extension of grace towards them. No-one can expect this extension to occur; they must expect the worst: 'this favor is not earned by works [that is, human actions] but comes from free calling', as Calvin succinctly puts it.[1] And 'free calling' comes from God, and God alone.

There would seem to be a logical contradiction between these two positions, but Calvinism refuses to admit this, arguing that since all humankind is guilty of original sin – Adam and Eve having doomed the human race forever in this respect – none of us can have any expectation at all of being saved. As Calvin asserts in rather chilling terms: 'man falls according as God's providence ordains, but he falls by his own fault.'[2] God is choosing to save some of us in spite of our collective guilt, if precious few, according to the theologians of the period. We must also understand that this guilt lasts for ever and ever, and can never be expiated, no matter what we may do. Regardless of how godly a life you may lead, the outcome is set in stone: the Calvinist God does not change his mind.

It is not at all surprising that those who subscribed to this theology went through psychological torments trying to decide what God's decision was in their individual cases. John Bunyan, a prominent Baptist, has left us a fascinating record of his struggles against what he perceived to be God's implacable will in his 'spiritual autobiography' of 1666, *Grace*

Abounding to the Chief of Sinners. The work's overall tone is very pessimistic: if few are to be saved, then why would he be one of them? Especially since, in line with the practice of Calvinist-based churches, he was required to keep scrutinizing his own conduct minutely for signs of God's grace having picked him out. At best, such signs tended to come and go, often very fleetingly, and it was in the nature of anything so dependent on the individual's psychological states that a positive sign was almost always followed by a negative, often triggering dramatic mood swings in such believers. Catholics had Confession to fall back upon as a way of unburdening themselves of their sins, and then atoning for them as instructed by their priestly confessor. At least in theory their guilt could be assuaged. Under a theology which had done away with a formal system of confession, however, Calvinists could only brood incessantly over their apparent sins, plunging them deeper into guilt.

Calvinist theology is based on a pessimistic assessment of the spiritual prospects for most of the human race. It encourages a stringently detailed form of introspection on the part of believers if they are to discover whether they might just be among the lucky few. Hope does exist, but not much. *Grace Abounding* records Bunyan's personal progress to what he assumed was a state of grace in the eyes of God. During this epic journey to what was known as the 'conversion experience' that constitutes the crux of the spiritual autobiographical form, Bunyan goes through a series of psychological highs and lows that shake him to the core of his being. (We might think of the conversion experience in modern terms as a particularly intense form of epiphany.) Close reading of the Bible can sometimes convince him that he is to be saved: 'Now was my heart filled full of comfort and hope, and now I could believe that my sins should be forgiven me.'[3] But such states are invariably short-lived, only to be followed by feelings of the utmost despair:

For about the space of a month after, a very great storm came down upon me, which handled me twenty times worse than all I had met with before: it came stealing upon me, now by one piece, then by another; first all my comfort was taken from me, then darkness seized upon me.[4]

It is a pattern that is to be repeated incessantly until the conversion experience occurs: 'Now did my chains fall off my Legs indeed, I was loosed from my afflictions and irons.'[5] These are the signs he has been waiting for: the signs that he is truly one of the elite who can look forward to salvation. Bunyan is never again to be put through the same torments after this point, but neither is he to be completely settled in his mind, reporting that even after becoming a lay preacher (a highly admired one capable of attracting large audiences, as we know from contemporary accounts), 'sometimes I should be assaulted with great discouragement' or with 'thoughts of blasphemy' when addressing his congregation.[6] And that is the problem with predestination: it cannot be conclusively confirmed one way or the other until after one's death, and that is hardly enough to dispel pessimism altogether. As one of the main characters in Bunyan's fictional tale *The Life and Death of Mr Badman*, a minister with firm predestinarian beliefs, warns of a sinner who dies quietly instead of in the state of fear his condition warrants:

no man can Judge of their eternall condition by the manner of any of these kinds of deaths. He that dies quietly, suddenly, or under consternation of spirit, may goe to Heaven, or may goe to Hell; no man can tell whether a man goes, by *any such* manner of death.[7]

In other words, there is always some doubt around to keep one's pessimism alive: it can never be shaken off entirely.

In Bunyan's most famous fictional work, *The Pilgrim's Progress*, the protagonist Christian is racked by doubt throughout the narrative's journey, and the psychological ups and downs alternate just as bewilderingly between elation and despair as they had in Bunyan's own life. Initially Christian is weighed down by a huge burden he must carry on his back, but when he sees an image of Christ on the cross before him on the road, the burden rolls off and he is overcome with joy: 'Then was *Christian* glad and lightsom, and said with a merry heart, *He has given me rest, by his sorrow; and life, by his death.*'[8] We might think his salvation is now assured, especially since the event is followed by the presentation of a certificate to him by an angel, to be handed in at the Heavenly City on arrival. Yet doubt continues to haunt him, and he is plunged into despair on many occasions thereafter, as when he and a companion, Hopeful, are captured by the fearsome Giant Despair and imprisoned in the dungeon of his castle – Doubting Castle. It is an experience that leaves Christian contemplating suicide, and it will not be until they have passed over the River of Death and reached the gates of the Heavenly City that Christian and Hopeful can be given the final verdict on their respective cases. Their tale has a happy ending: they are welcomed in. Another acquaintance met with on the road, however, is not so fortunate. Ignorance, who had simply assumed that a blameless life, such as the one he assures us he has led, would gain him entry despite the fact that he had never received a certificate, is cast down 'to Hell, even from the Gates of Heaven'.[9] No man indeed knows his fate, until it is too late for him to rest content in this life.

This obsession with predestination carries over into the wider world of fiction in the eighteenth century. Spiritual autobiography lies behind the work of Daniel Defoe, for example, who is usually regarded as the first proper novelist in English. Defoe is likely to have been familiar with the ideas of Calvinism since, like Bunyan, he had come from a sectarian, Nonconformist background. Defoe adopts the framework of the spiritual autobiography as a structuring device for his most famous work of fiction, *Robinson Crusoe*, which, as many scholars have pointed out, contains numerous echoes of *The Pilgrim's Progress* throughout the narrative (Crusoe calls the island he is shipwrecked upon 'Despair', recalling Giant Despair in Bunyan, for example). He goes on to employ the same form of narrative structure in several other works, helping to entrench the spiritual autobiographical form firmly within the tradition of the English novel.

Robinson Crusoe features the same series of dramatic mood swings between hope and desperation that we find in *The Pilgrim's Progress* as the narrative unfolds, with the character isolated not just by his anxieties but physically, on a deserted island thousands of miles from home. There is even an approximation of a conversion experience, when a particular passage from the Bible is enough to convince Crusoe that God can be relied upon to look after him in his troubles:

> reading the Scripture, I came to these Words, *He is exalted a Prince and a Saviour, to give Repentance, and to give Remission*: I threw down the Book, and with my Heart as well as my Hands lifted up to Heaven, in a Kind of Extasy of Joy, I cry'd out aloud, *Jesus, thou Son of* David, *Jesus, thou exalted Prince and Saviour, give me Repentance!*[10]

The story does not end at that point, however, and in the characteristic manner of spiritual autobiography, Crusoe is to experience many other dark nights of the soul when he wonders about his fate and whether he will be saved.

The shadowy H. F., the hero of Defoe's *A Journal of the Plague Year*, also undergoes the tribulations of the spiritual autobiographical lifestyle. He has to contend with the plague raging all around him in London in the 1660s without ever knowing if he is going to be allowed by God to survive. It is a powerful metaphor for the division that Calvinist theology insists will be made by God between the saved and the damned, with the unfortunate – we are being invited to assume damned – victims being cut down mercilessly on all sides. The mortality figures are reported by H. F. in the tone of one who fully expects to become yet another such statistic at a moment's notice, as so many of his neighbours are doing. H. F. does survive, but only after a protracted long dark night of the soul, fearful of his fate. As we know from the historical record, the plague has merely abated and can, and will, return in due course (outbreaks were continuing well into the eighteenth century). Safety is never finally to be assured, therefore, no matter how many signs we may feel we have received hinting at the likelihood of a positive outcome.

H. F. decides at an early stage in the narrative that he will not flee the city to escape the plague, as it is in God's power to ensure 'that he could cause his Justice to overtake me when and where he thought fit' in any case.[11] Paradoxically enough, he feels able to distinguish between his conduct and that of 'the Turks and Mahometans in Asia' who, 'presuming upon their professed predestinating notions, and of every man's end being predetermined and unalterably beforehand decreed . . . would go unconcerned into infected places and converse with infected persons, by which means they died at the rate of ten or fifteen thousand a week'.[12] The tortuousness of Calvinist reasoning is prominently on display at such points, and for an outsider it can be difficult to distinguish between the two religious viewpoints.

Defoe's last novel, *Roxana*, however, tells a very different story, dealing with someone who does not even experience the limited comfort that the Calvinist outlook can provide intermittently. This is Calvinism seen from the other side of the spiritual divide between the saved and the damned. Roxana's lifestyle as a courtesan to a series of rich and powerful men more than hints at her being a candidate for damnation, as does her systematic farming out of her unwanted children resulting from her many liaisons. She may have the odd twinge of conscience about her abnegation of parental responsibility, but not enough to change her ways, nor her mercenary pursuit of wealth through the gifts of her many lovers. It is only when a lost daughter returns to upset her lifestyle that she is forced to face up to the consequences of her actions, and her solution to the problem that the daughter, Susan, poses for her is shocking in its lack of compassion. Whether at Roxana's behest or not, Susan is probably murdered – most likely by Roxana's loyal servant, Amy. It is left tantalizingly open, but Roxana's attack of conscience afterwards is highly suggestive of guilt. She even blames the event for the collapse in her fortunes from then on: 'the Blast of Heaven seem'd to follow the Injury done the poor Girl, by us both; and I was brought so low again, that my Repentance seem'd to be only the Consequence of my Misery, as my Misery was of my Crime.'[13] We are left with the image of someone utterly consumed by guilt: the ultimate fate of the damned, as envisaged by Calvinist doctrine.

A later author who dealt with Calvinism, this time in order to be pessimistic about its effect on believers, was the Scots author James Hogg, whose early nineteenth-century novel *The Private Memoirs and Confessions of a Justified Sinner* reads like an inverted *Pilgrim's Progress* (the latter is even mentioned at one point in the narrative). The tale is set in the early eighteenth century, when passions about religion ran high in Scotland. Hogg is particularly successful at capturing the dangers of the predestinarian outlook. What if you were able to convince yourself that you were definitely a member of the elite to be saved? What actions might this lead you to feel completely justified in undertaking? How extreme might these turn out to be? In the case of its protagonist, Robert Wringhim, the answer is murder, because if you are of the elite then you cannot sin: all your actions must be considered justified by God.

Wringhim is the unacknowledged illegitimate son of a Calvinist preacher, the Reverend Wringhim, his mother's spiritual director. Robert takes the Reverend's name after his ostensible father effectively disowns him, suspecting his wife's infidelity with the 'flaming predestinarian divine'.[14] The Reverend imbues Robert with predestinarianism to the extent of assuring him as a youth that he is undoubtedly one of the chosen few whose destiny cannot be altered by anything they do. The conversion experience is more or less handed to Robert on a plate, but it has as profound an impact on him as it did on Bunyan before. Robert later encounters a figure he is amazed to find is his mirror image, a figure few in his circle of acquaintances ever seem able to catch sight of clearly. Gil-Martin, as he introduces himself, persuades Robert to take his certainty of being a 'justified' individual quite literally: to assume that whatever he does cannot in any way affect his salvation. Robert has already decided that his purpose in life is to punish those unworthy of salvation on behalf of God, and he carries this belief to the logical conclusion of killing them: 'I conceived it decreed, not that I should be a minister of the gospel, but a champion of it, to cut off the enemies of the Lord, from the face of the earth.'[15]

The unsaveable even appear to extend to the ranks of those with a reputation for piety, such as another of the local residents, Mr Blanchard, who reveals his status by accusing Robert of 'carrying your ideas of absolute predestination, and its concomitant appendages, to an extent that overthrows all religion and revelation altogether'.[16] That is always a distinct possibility with such a divisive doctrine, and one only too easy for the zealot to fall into. With Blanchard duly 'cut off', Gil-Martin eggs Robert on to ever more outrageous actions, probably even involving the murder of his own mother, but Robert never retains any memory of these events afterwards.

It will not be until the point of death that he begins to doubt the truth of his salvation, proceeding to hang himself, quite possibly at Gil-Martin's command: 'My hour is at hand. – Almighty God, what is this that I am about to do! The hour of repentance is past, and now my fate is inevitable.'[17]

As an indictment of the Calvinist mindset, *Confessions* is devastating. Hogg was himself raised in this tradition, Calvinism being strong within Scottish religious life (as it still is), yet by demonstrating how it could be interpreted if taken literally, he is raising awkward questions about the value of predestination. This is pessimism towards the belief rather than because of it; an intellectualized reaction as opposed to Bunyan's emotional one.

Pessimism about one's prospects seemed to be the fate of Calvinists in general, given that the system they laboured under has all the appearance of a lottery. Of course the odds are almost punitively stacked against any one individual being the winner in this situation. Nevertheless one had no alternative but to go on examining one's behaviour and thoughts in painstaking detail on the off-chance that against all probability, and your own ingrained sinning nature inherited from Adam and Eve, it might just be you after all – that the positive signs would eventually outweigh the negative. (Not for nothing was 'precise' one of the descriptions of the Calvinist temperament during the period.) Lotteries do have some winners. It seems like a recipe for intense psychological suffering on a lifelong scale. Bunyan himself is constantly reduced to a state of helpless despair, almost unable to function in the everyday world, so pessimistic does he become about his spiritual prospects. The 'worst' looms horribly large and vivid in his imagination.

* ❋ *

As noted earlier, Islam is often viewed in the West as a fatalistic religion – one that encourages its adherents to believe that whatever happens is God's will, and that nothing they do can affect how events will turn out. They must just resign themselves to it. The lead character in Hilary Mantel's novel *Eight Months on Ghazzah Street*, Frances Shore, resident in Jeddah while her husband Andrew is stationed there, is appalled by the reckless driving habits she observes in the city. Seeing children being allowed to clamber all over the seats in speeding cars, despite numerous signs about road safety posted along the highway, she asks Andrew, 'Haven't they heard of seatbelts?', to which he replies, 'Bit of a dodgy concept . . . Allah has appointed a term to every life.'[18] From a Western point of view, that constitutes fatalism, but to Islamic believers it is in keeping with what the Qur'an tells them. Throughout the Qur'an the necessity for submission to Allah is emphasized, because he is guiding the actions of everyone: 'If Allah afflicts you with a misfortune none can remove it but He; and if He bestows on you a favour, none can withhold His bounty. He is bountiful to whom He will.'[19]

It is worth giving some consideration to whether fatalism is all that qualitatively different from Christian predestination, however, since both insist that the world operates according to a divinely constructed master plan that cannot be altered by any human action. God wills what human fate will be, and the individual is merely an instrument for this. As far as the Calvinist is concerned, he is either saved or damned and that decision is totally immutable. For the Islamic drivers in Jeddah in Mantel's novel, it is a waste of time complying with safety precautions, since their fate, too, is preordained: Allah 'is bountiful to whom He will'. A seat belt will not save you if your allotted term has run out. The big difference is that predestination lets you glimpse, even if only fleetingly and with all sorts of psychological complications and qualifications, what that decision might be in your individual instance through scrutinizing your own conduct closely ('might' being the operative word, however) – if you are lucky enough to be a member of the saved, that is. The damned must remain in blissful ignorance, not being vouchsafed such critical insights by God. With fatalism, on the other hand, you just assume that there is no point in looking into this at all, because what will be will be. The Qur'an's rationale for this is as follows: 'Every misfortune that befalls the earth, or your own persons, is ordained before We bring it into being. That is easy for Allah: so that you may not grieve for the good things you miss or be overjoyed at what you gain.'[20] This means that you cannot read too much into whatever happens to you. The Calvinist, however, is being positively urged to interpret both what he or she loses and gains as signs pointing towards a particular outcome.

Neither Islam nor Christianity believe that there is anything you can do to alter your fate. Predestination, however, adds in a layer of anxiety to religion that, as we know from Bunyan's experience, can be psychologically destabilizing even to the most devout believer. Fatalism, at least in principle, can largely remove your worries about your fate, because you must simply accept it as it proceeds to unfold. One does sound more conducive to the development of feelings of pessimism than the other, although in the stricter sense it would have to be said that both are essentially deterministic in orientation, allowing no exception to the rule – the rule as set down by God, crucially. Whether it always works out quite so neatly in practice is much more problematical: religion has a way of preying on believers' fears, and in every case it does depend on how you interpret the relevant holy book. Christian drivers may well abide by safety precautions, but they do not believe this will alter God's decision on their individual fates: they too are at God's mercy, seat belt or not.

* * *

Entropy is a theory that has featured prominently in both religious and scientific thought. The belief that the world had a limited life cycle, and that it was now in the process of inexorably running down, was widely held in the medieval and early modern eras in Europe. At the end of that cycle would come the apocalyptic Judgement Day promised in the Bible (as in the Book of Revelation), when the ultimate division between the saved and the damned would be made by God. That would be the final curtain for humanity. Millenarian thought insisted that this was imminent, and millenarianism was rife in sixteenth- and seventeenth-century England, with various dates being set for the end of the world at God's hands. Present-day evangelicals, particularly in America, are still engaged in this activity, returning to the Bible on each occasion their prediction proves to be wrong to check their chronology, and invariably managing to come up with new dates for Judgement Day (or 'the Rapture', as they have taken to calling the event), when the saved elite will be swept straight up to heaven. Millenarianism dies hard in the more fundamentalist versions of Protestantism, and pessimism about one's prospects must prey on many believers' minds when contemplating the coming of 'the Rapture'.

A favourite trope of Renaissance poetry was to compare the individual's life to the diurnal sequence. The sun's passage through the heavens marked the various stages of life's journey, with early morning signalling childhood, noon the prime of life, and everything from then on as the progress through maturity and old age to death. Andrew Marvell therefore warns his 'Coy Mistress' that they must take advantage of their youth, because 'we cannot make our Sun / Stand still'.[21] The day itself taught us that everything was finite, as George Herbert emphasized:

Sweet day, so cool, so calm, so bright,
The bridall of the earth and skie:
The dew shall weep thy fall to night;
    For thou must die.[22]

The seasons formed another useful symbol for the process, with spring as childhood, and so on through the year (we still speak of people being in 'the autumn of their years'). John Donne combines daily and annual cycles when he refers to the shortest day of the year as 'the year's midnight'.[23] Again, this relies on the concept of entropy: of finite lifespans for every aspect of divine creation, with mankind just a microcosm of the larger sequence played out in the natural world day by day, year by year. The seasons may renew themselves in a way that human beings cannot (although Christian belief did promise an afterlife in heaven), but even the natural world can only last as long as God has dictated: a doomsday clock presides over all creation.

Scientific entropy also posits a limited lifetime for the universe, if one of significantly longer duration than theology tended to suggest, running into billions of years. In this case, it is dependent on the natural processes at work in both our solar system and the universe as a whole. The sun is steadily using up its energy and eventually will burn out altogether. It will turn into a red giant star, scorching the inner planets in the first instance, then declining from there into a black dwarf star no longer radiating life-giving heat and light out towards the earth. The result will be that the solar system will no longer be able to support life. Yet more problems emerge from the effect of the continuing expansion of the universe set in motion by the Big Bang, which will drive galaxies ever further apart, creating an even more inhospitable environment for the development of stars. Some scientists have speculated that a possible outcome of this relentless expansion might be a 'Big Crunch', the mirror image of the Big Bang that created the universe in the first place. So the universe may have a limited lifespan too, or at least the universe as we have always known it; there has been speculation as to the possibility of a 'Big Bounce' following on from a 'Big Crunch', creating yet another universe after the current one disappears. Another theory is that the effect of continued expansion will be a 'Big Rip', where all the universe's stars are torn apart. Whatever the outcome may be, it is not going to be good news for humanity.

One theory that did seem to promise an eternally existing cosmos, however, was the 'bubble multiverse', which truly does sound like the world of science fiction. This posits 'that our universe is just one of an ever-inflating multitude of discrete "bubble" universes. These bubbles are eternally budding off new universes even as individual universes age and die.'[24] This budding was caused by the massive 'inflation' of the universe's size which occurred an infinitesimal instant after the Big Bang, and it was held to go on creating new bubbles out of the old ones into infinity. Whatever comfort humanity might have taken from this (a matter for metaphysical speculation, one suspects), even this theory is now being challenged by a group of American scientists whose claim is that inflation did in fact come to an end after creating a 'branching multiverse', which is therefore finite.[25] No good news forthcoming here either, it would appear: the doomsday clock strikes yet again.

There are many theories in current physics capable, in what they are saying about the structure of the universe, of giving those outside the field considerable pause for thought, since they have wide-ranging implications for our view of ourselves. Chaos theory and complexity theory both show the limits of human power, of what we can and cannot control in our lives. In chaos theory, systems are seen to operate in a way we cannot manipulate, obeying laws that are deeply mysterious ('strange attractors', for example, which direct their operation). Nature is made up of a series of interacting, interlocking systems that are often pitched at 'the edge of chaos', just managing to maintain a sense of equilibrium. Sometimes this equilibrium cannot be maintained and the systems slide into a state of chaos; that is, unpredictable behaviour ('randomness' to a scientist). There is what has been referred to as the 'butterfly effect', where small effects at one point in a system can cause huge changes at a much larger scale: the beating of a butterfly's wings at one location creating a cascade of events leading to a typhoon in another part of the globe, perhaps. Human beings are simply at the mercy of such phenomena, with their hidden structures. Some theorists have argued that the stock market should be treated that way, as an inherently unstable system prone to unpredictable swings, no matter what its apologists may say. Benoit Mandelbrot, noted for his pioneering work on fractal geometry, emphasized this aspect of financial trading, where 'rational behavior on the part of the market may lead to "wild" speculative bubbles' – something with which we have all become only too familiar in recent years.[26]

In complexity theory, systems are held to have the power to self-organize themselves to higher levels of efficiency, suggesting yet more limits to the range of human power. In effect, we do not know what is driving the doomsday clock, nor what it means for us as a species. What these theories are telling us ought to make us wary of tinkering too deeply with the workings of systems and possibly projecting ourselves inadvertently into chaos – as many believe is happening right now with climate change. But it would be very optimistic to believe that human beings will refrain from doing so. Perhaps we are under the spell of our own particular strange attractor? (As far as the oil companies go, that would appear to be profit.)

The ecology movement also sees the doomsday clock as ticking down, with humankind responsible for creating the situation. Some of its more extreme voices are completely pessimistic about what faces us as a species, thanks to our reckless over-exploitation of the environment. We have no-one but ourselves to blame for the global warming crisis. James Lovelock, for example, has issued some dire warnings about the prospects for humanity on a rapidly warming planet, which is seemingly inexorably heading towards a critical tipping point that will change the way we live forever. He foresees the possibility of the human race being reduced to only a few thousand people living at subsistence level in the polar regions. This is about as pessimistic an assessment as one will find about our current prospects in a growth-obsessed culture. Lovelock is precisely the kind of figure who riles denialists; to them, his views are doom-mongering on a grand scale.

Lovelock is unconvinced that we can leave it to science to extricate us from what for him is a worsening situation that is heading towards an apocalyptic conclusion – and one that may not be all that long in arriving. The Earth is 'Gaia', a delicately balanced living organism, and to Lovelock it is now desperately sick. Humankind is only succeeding in making its condition worse. Although he has suggested some remedies, Lovelock is not at all optimistic that we can prevent the worst scenario from occurring: we are about to experience 'Gaia's revenge', and it will be harsh. It begins to sound a bit like a 'revenge tragedy', and revenge tragedies always end badly – as we shall go on to see in chapter Five.

Lovelock popularized the Gaia principle, which has been picked up by many other groups in the ecology movement, although others do not necessarily think that all is lost. Greens think the way to halt the slide is to reduce the Earth's population (very significantly in some projections, down to a mere fraction of what it is, at just over seven billion and rising) and to consume far less than we are doing; perhaps even to strive to return to a pre-industrial culture that would give the Earth the opportunity to recover from its sickness. Pessimism abounds in this area, and that is entirely under-standable given the general reluctance on the part of the advanced nations to cut back on their standard of living. Vague promises are made (the Kyoto Protocols to cut carbon emissions, for example), but rarely abided by and at best indif-ferently monitored. Agreement in principle about what should be done is about the best that ever happens. Some nations (Australia, for example) even refuse to accept that, or to sign up to any document specifying when it should be achieved – although so far such targets have never been met. The general public keeps track of these debates over Gaia's health, and our potential fate as a species, with a sort of horrified fascination. Doomsday stories are always guaranteed to find press coverage and an audience. Yet despite their impact we continue to vote for political parties who are committed to the concept of growthism.

* * *

Although it is not always defined as such, melancholy is a condition that has existed throughout human history in some form or other: it is mentioned in literature as far back as Aristotle. Yet it does seem to have become a far more prominent feature of European culture from the modern period onwards. No doubt the notion of the universe running down, and possibly even entering its final stages (as millenarianism confidently kept claiming), contributed to this development to some extent. The condition was originally thought, however, to derive from a physical source, one of the four main 'humours' that the body contained – black bile, phlegm, blood, yellow bile. These formed a person's character, making one melancholic, phlegmatic, sanguine or choleric, respectively. From the sixteenth through the eighteenth centuries, melancholy was a widely experienced and talked-about phenomenon, attracting much attention from the medical profession of the time, and becoming a rich source of material for many writers – not to mention a rich source of income for several generations of doctors. One of the things that Shakespeare's *Hamlet* does is to present us with a study of melancholy in the person of its lead character, and many other poets and creative artists of the period were fascinated by the condition and how it affects human behaviour.

Robert Burton's monumental *The Anatomy of Melancholy* (1621) is one of the first detailed attempts to classify what the condition involves. Burton, who was described by one of his editors as 'a good-humoured pessimist', broke melancholy down into various types, from the relatively mild through to the severe.[27] The causes are multiple (sorrow, anger, assorted cares and miseries, idleness, solitariness, climate, even bad air and witches), as are the cures. The level of black bile in the individual's system could be critical: the greater the imbalance with the other humours, the more intense the feelings of melancholy would become. As Burton put it: 'our body is like a clock; if one wheel be amiss, all the rest are disordered.'[28] The eighteenth-century physician George Cheyne went so far as to call melancholy 'the English Malady' in his study of that name, as if the inhabitants of the British Isles were particularly prone to develop that kind of temperament.[29]

Nowadays we tend to see melancholy as a precursor to what we call depression, and in many of the reported cases in the earlier medical literature, that would indeed be the diagnosis put forward for such symptoms today. Detailed descriptions of the symptoms to look out for are given in the current (fifth) edition of the American Psychiatric Association's *Diagnostic and Statistical Manual of Mental Disorders*, also known as DSM-5 (2013). Bunyan's autobiography strongly suggests that he would be a prime candidate for such a diagnosis, with his powerfully documented psychological highs and lows suggesting a bipolar personality. Far more of the latter than the former prove to be in evidence in his narrative: 'Now was the battle won, and down fell I, as a bird that is shot from the top of a tree, into great guilt and fearful despair', being but one of many striking examples to be found.[30]

The medical profession in the eighteenth century was particularly interested in melancholy, and devised many treatments for it. As Allan Ingram notes: 'because this was an age of medical laissez-faire, both physicians and quacks offered and championed a staggering range of treatments for melancholy conditions, some of them plausible, but many of them, one would think, dangerous and even life-threatening.'[31] It even came to be regarded as a 'fashionable' disease, almost turning into a form of epidemic among the upper classes in consequence: 'for much of the period, melancholy was frothily fashionable, a condition that often seemed less of an illness and more of a blessing for the budding poet, wilting lady wishing to show off her latest nightdress, or anyone who desired to seem in the slightest bit sensitive or clever.'[32] The afflicted from that social class conscientiously tried out the treatments their physicians recommended, whether or not they were plausible – or dangerous.

Viewed from a modern perspective, melancholy describes a spectrum of conditions from severe depression at the one end to sadness at the other. There was certainly a pessimistic cast to the experience of melancholy, a sense that a life mainly made up of unremitting worry and trouble lay ahead of one. The novelist Henry Fielding reports his wife Charlotte giving vent to a heart-rending example of this when, on the birth of a daughter, she exclaimed, 'Good God! have I produced a Creature who is to undergo what I have suffered!'[33] We might be inclined to interpret this now as the very early onset of post-natal depression, but in the period it was more likely to signal melancholy. However it is classified, it is an expression of a deeply pessimistic temperament.

* * *

War and humankind's urge to violence have generated pessimistic attitudes about human nature, as well as heated debates about whether or not this is our true nature or whether we are capable of developing past this kind of behaviour. The jury is still out on that, but war does seem to bring out some of the very worst traits of humanity, as well as, paradoxically enough, some of the most admirable: cruelty on the one hand, compassion for the victims on the other. Yet it is the worst that sticks in the mind when one is faced with the sheer scale of the cruelty and suffering in the Second World War, with the Holocaust marking some sort of nadir of man's inhumanity to man. Genocide on that scale – an estimated six million dead – is extremely difficult to comprehend. The German philosopher Theodor W. Adorno was even moved to declare that 'to write poetry after Auschwitz is barbaric', that in fact 'it has become impossible to write poetry today', and the history of fascism continues to cast a long shadow into our own time.[34] Racist hatred has certainly not gone away; nor has ethnic cleansing. Openly fascist and proto-fascist parties keep emerging throughout Europe, and still find zealous supporters.

Millions of casualties were recorded in combat in both the First and Second World Wars. The numbers far exceeded anything previously experienced in history. The burst of patriotic fervour that had been sparked by the outbreak of the First World War began to wear very thin well before its end, as the losses on both sides mounted to unprecedented levels and the reality of what was happening began to sink in. Poets caught up in the fighting were particularly sensitive to the air of disenchantment that developed as the war rolled on and the death-toll grew remorselessly, and the poetry they produced in response to their experiences can be painful to read. Glorification of war has become far less common since then, and is associated in the popular mind with warmongering. The Nazi movement glorified war, and that was taken to be proof enough of its evil intent to countries still scarred by the experience of 1914–18. References to the gloriousness of war tend to be avoided in countries like ours these days and are likely to ring alarm bells if they ever do appear. When the character of Colonel Kilgore in the film *Apocalypse Now* (dir. Francis Ford Coppola, 1979) tells us that 'I love the smell of napalm in the morning', and that it signals 'victory' to him, we are alerted to the dubiousness of America's role in the Vietnam War – or at least we should be, given the horrific effects of napalm on both people and the environment. The suffering and desecration that inevitably come in war's wake tend to be brought to public attention far more than it used to be. We are all well used to seeing unsavoury images of war on the broadcast news nowadays, and these are always presented in a sober fashion meant to inspire reflection on humanity's dark side rather than to glamorize conflict in any way.

There is a notable exception to this attitude towards war in the contemporary world that is worth mentioning, however, and that is Islamic jihad, or 'holy war'. This is glorified by groups like al-Qaeda and Isis, who present it as every Muslim's duty to subscribe to the concept. The recruiting videos they are increasingly producing make that point forcefully. It is a claim that can be backed up by reference to the Qur'an, which asserts, for example, that 'Allah loves those who fight for His cause in ranks as firm as a mighty edifice', and is full of injunctions to punish the unbelievers.[35] The vast majority of Muslims interpret the notion in a far less dramatic way than that, however, more along the lines of 'defending one's religion', and could not be described as adherents of terrorism. This is a tricky topic to discuss from a Western perspective, since one must take into account the depth of opposition to the West in Islamic countries and the emotions it can arouse – and legitimately so. There is a long history of Western imperialism, both political and economic, lying behind this, as well as the Christian version of holy war, which the Western powers fully supported as their way of bringing 'civilization' to the rest of the world in their colonizing days. It does not pay to become too sanctimonious about the reaction jihad has unleashed in the modern world. That said, it nevertheless induces pessimism in demonstrating the lengths that religions can push believers to in asserting what for them is the only received 'truth'. The assumption of superiority that drives such campaigns cannot accept dissenting views, and it has been the cause of untold suffering and human misery down through the years. The fact that such an assumption is still widely held merely confirms the pessimist in his or her worldview: human nature does not come out of this very well either.

At its worst, which has happened on many occasions throughout history from both the Christian and Islamic sides, the zealotry inspired by the notion of holy war can mean attempting to eradicate other religions altogether. Monotheism has much to answer for in that sense, and does not in the main generate much in the way of optimism about humanity's ability to tolerate other worldviews and to agree to disagree when it comes to matters of belief. At best, monotheisms will grudgingly accept each other's existence, but still adhere to the principle that only they are in possession of the received truth. Other believers tend to be viewed mainly as potential converts.

Violence and taking up arms is also often glorified to a certain extent when political revolutions break out. Revolutions provide further evidence as to how difficult human beings can find it to work out a compromise with other worldviews, since they generally constitute an act of desperation on the part of those who feel oppressed or marginalized by an authoritarian government. That it has to come to violence to register such grievances is a sad comment on the corrupting effect of political power. Pessimists would observe that oppressing others is all too common a human trait, and surveying history reveals numerous examples of it in action. Authoritarianism is more the rule than the exception. As if to confirm just how easily power can corrupt, revolutions have an unfortunate tendency to turn into authoritarian regimes themselves, as did the Russian Revolution of 1917 (although it is by no means unique in that respect).

The historian Ian Morris's argument in *War! What Is It Good For?*, that war has its good points in terms of technological progress and that war's casualties can be offset by population gains made elsewhere on the globe, are worth remembering in this context. The closing speech in Tom Stoppard's comic play *Jumpers*, delivered by the deeply cynical university vice chancellor Archie Jumper, offers up a thought-provoking balance sheet of what a view like Morris's requires us to accept:

> Do not despair – many are happy much of the time; more eat than starve, more are healthy than sick, more curable than dying; not so many dying as dead; and one of the thieves was saved. Hell's bells and all's well – half the world is at peace with itself, and so is the other half; vast areas are unpolluted; millions of children grow up without suffering deprivation, and millions, while deprived, grow up without suffering cruelties, and millions, while deprived and cruelly treated, none the less grow up.[36]

Optimists would probably think this was reason enough to look to the future with hope; that somehow or other humanity will muddle through. Pessimists, however, would respond to the passage's cynicism and thinly veiled sarcasm in a very different manner, wondering what the continued existence of starvation, deprivation and cruelty in the modern age says about the human race: in other words, just how willing are we to shrug our shoulders at 'collateral damage'? War brings such phenomena into sharp focus, and again,what you make of it all is very much in the eye of the beholder. Stoppard's black humour yields some sobering thoughts that invite us to examine our worldview. It holds Leibniz's claim that we live in 'the best of all possible worlds' up for scrutiny, making clear just how bad a deal it represents for much of humanity.[37] At least implicitly, most of us do think somewhat like Archie, but whether it provides adequate justification for optimism is a debatable point. It is the kind of metaphysical dilemma in which Samuel Beckett's work consistently leaves us.

* ✳ *

Crime is a constant factor in the evolution of society, hence the institutions that have been developed to cope with its impact on the general public. It could be said that the very existence of a legal system and a police force represents an overall pessimistic assessment of human nature – an acknowledgement that humanity at large can only be trusted so far. The underlying rationale for the creation of these systems is that without the safeguards they provide, the incidence of criminal behaviour would most likely soar, putting all of us at greater risk from theft, criminal violence and so on (as does tend to happen if civil order ever breaks down, even if only temporarily, as in urban riots). Prisons stand witness to the fact that even with such safeguards, transgressions will nevertheless occur and just have to be accepted as a part of life. The ways in which prisons in different countries treat offenders vary quite considerably around the globe, from the relatively lenient and rehabilitation-oriented to the harsh and overtly punitive (the death penalty still applies in many places, in several American states no less than in the non-Western world), but no society to date has ever succeeded in eradicating crime, nor the impulse to commit it. Nor has the public fascination with crime ever gone away. Bookstores in the West, for example, groan under the weight of the crime fiction volumes on their shelves.

Anarchists, however, have argued that crime would die out if society was organized along the lines they propose; that with minimum regulation and the absence of the authoritarian powers of the modern state – complete with police forces and armies to reinforce this – humanity would change for the better. One of the first theorists of anarchism was William Godwin, who argued that crime, and anti-social conduct in general, could be kept at bay if we were all vigilant in observing our fellow citizens, passing on any criticisms we might have of their actions. The 'observant eye, of public judgement' would, Godwin thought, be enough to make us act responsibly and bear the public good in mind at all times.[38] Libertarians tend to argue on similar lines to anarchists, if perhaps without the same overall idealistic intent, claiming that human beings can be trusted to live without excessive rules and regulations (the 'nanny state' as it is called by such critics), and that the worst-case scenarios cited by sceptics as probable outcomes of significant deregulation just would not come about. The evidence for this is, however, thin at best (just as it is for Godwin's programme of public inspection). We only need to look at what has happened as a result of the systematic 'liberation' of financial markets from government-imposed regulation over the last few decades: the credit crash of 2007–8, from which the world economy is having considerable difficulty recovering. Undaunted, neo-liberal economists are still preaching the same message to governments, but the evidence against trusting human nature when it comes to matters like personal gain is not thin in this instance: it is only too plentiful. Why any libertarian or anarchistic society would fail to avoid a similar fate has to remain a mystery.

The more idealistic Marxists theorists also believed that the perfect society that would come about when communism was triumphant, the so-called Marxist 'utopia', would eliminate crime because everyone would be sharing equally in the production of that society, on the basis of the principle: 'From each according to his ability, to each according to his needs!'[39] There would be no basis for envy, so criminal activity would simply wither away in the resulting egalitarian culture. Whereas 'standard Marxist analysis would say that the workers are so alienated from their human nature that some of them turn to crime; and the objectives of the crime might be to defend the human values of their families', the need for this would disappear under a Marxist system.[40] Yet no communist country has ever managed to do without a police force, a legal system or a complex security system (invariably authoritarian in its operation). Unless we are willing to believe that crime in communist countries is nothing more than the residue of bourgeois capitalism, we have to conclude that this is yet another instance of a misplaced optimism about human nature. Neither is labour the only possible source of alienation; it can arise from many other aspects of our lives. These include emotional setbacks of almost any kind, for example – just talk to any adolescent.

War, as we shall see in chapters Five and Six, has also provoked an impassioned response from many authors, painters and filmmakers, particularly from the First World War onwards. The continual incidence of war, and its ever-present attendant 'collateral damage', is surely a reason for pessimism.

* ✳ *

Western society is based on the premise that human behaviour can be improved, and underpinning our educational, political and legal systems is a belief that we can be turned into responsible citizens who respect the rights of others and abide by the rule of law. There would be little point in educating people or imposing sanctions on law-breakers if we were unable to regulate our conduct. But there are theories that undermine this view in rather worrying ways: genetic determinism, for example. Genetic determinists argue that we are the product of a genetic make-up which we cannot override (or can override only to some limited extent), and that this disposes us towards particular types of behaviour – sometimes of an antisocial kind.

Hans J. Eysenck's name is often mentioned in this context, for his work on the relationship between genetics and IQ, from which he draws conclusions that have proved to be highly contentious. Many of his critics consider them racist.

Eysenck's argument was that the weight of evidence pointed to the 'overwhelming importance of genetic factors in producing the great variety of intellectual differences which we observe in our culture, and much of the difference observed between certain racial groups'.[41] To state it that way was to imply that it was just part of the order of things, something we had to accept as a fact of life. As far as the nature/nurture debate is concerned, Eysenck appears to be firmly on the side of nature, meaning that the differences between races to which he draws attention are to be considered entirely natural and in effect unalterable. The many other factors that may have contributed to such findings – environment, educational and employment opportunities, economic and social status, the landscape of nurture in general – are taken to be of far less importance by the genetic determinist. One can easily see the ammunition this provides to the far right, who are only too receptive to such conclusions, which appear almost to justify discrimination. From that perspective, money spent on trying to ensure equal opportunities is money wasted.

Feminist theory can also take on a determinist slant on occasion, arguing that the sexes are biologically programmed to act in one way or another, and that this just has to be accepted as a fact of life. Carried to an extreme, such views can justify what has come to be known as 'separatist feminism', which advocates the withdrawal of women from a male-dominated society on the grounds that men will not, indeed cannot, change. To the separatist, there isn't even the glimmer of a possibility of this eventuality, and the pessimist would be the first to admit that there is a weight of historical evidence to back this up. Society will therefore always be patronizing and unfair towards women, refusing to treat them as equals to men. Men's natural tendency, built into their genetic make-up, as it were, is to be aggressive and domineering, and women should give up trying to alter this. Theorists like Hélène Cixous and Luce Irigaray have made a strong case for separatism, and it also informs the fiction of Monique Wittig.

Cixous's belief in the unbridgeable gap between the sexes can be seen to particular effect in her concept of *écriture féminine*, which argues that male and female writing are so different in approach and concerns that they cannot really be understood by those on the other side of the gender divide. Hence her conception of what 'women's writing' must be: 'Woman must write her self: must write about women and bring women to writing, from which they have been driven away as violently as from their bodies . . . I write woman: woman must write woman. And man, man.'[42] This is a recipe for separatism: what amounts to a justification of gender apartheid. Apart from anything else, it seems to throw into doubt the efforts of centuries of literary production, by both men and women, which has sought very sincerely to come to an understanding of both male and female behaviour and experience. One would be forced to conclude that they were collectively misguided. Luce Irigaray also takes a firmly separatist line in her writings. Women are so qualitatively different from men, in her opinion, that men will never be able to fathom them: 'It is useless', she argues, 'to trap women in the exact definition of what they mean, to make them repeat (themselves) so that it will be clear . . . And if you ask them insistently what they are thinking about, they can only reply: Nothing. Everything.'[43] Women are much more complex creatures than men, therefore: biology dictates that, and Irigaray objects strongly to women being used primarily as a 'prop for the enactment of man's fantasies'.[44] Neither does she have much time for campaigns to bring about equal rights for women, feeling that something much more fundamental is needed: a 'revolution in thought and ethics' that would enable women to develop in the way their sexual difference plainly demands.[45] Until then, separatism would seem to be the only answer, and Irigaray is at best lukewarm about the possibility of such a revolution ever coming to pass: in the majority anyway, men could not make such an imaginative leap. It is a decidedly pessimistic vision of human affairs in which the worst is seen as by far the likeliest thing to happen – as it has so repeatedly in the past in women's experience.

Monique Wittig's work celebrates lesbian feminism. Her novel *Les Guérillères* pictures a world where strong-minded women exercise a control over their environment – including the male sex – that they are never able to aspire to within the confines of a patriarchal society. Interestingly enough, they see the need to develop a warlike character in order to achieve their aims, refusing to be submissive any longer and engaging in open conflict with men:

> The women are on the ridges that command the pass. In this strategic position which is all to their advantage they draw their bows and fire thousands of arrows. Then the army breaks ranks. The men all begin to run in the greatest confusion . . . They jostle and collide with each other as they flee, they stumble over the bodies of the dead and wounded . . . Some climb on the hills making signs of surrender, they are soon slaughtered.[46]

This is the war of the sexes interpreted quite literally, and the author's relish in doing so is plain to see.

One can find female pessimism about patriarchy being strongly expressed in literature well before the rise of *écriture féminine*, however, as in the work of the eighteenth-century novelist Frances (Fanny) Burney. Over the course of her four novels, Burney's heroines are made progressively more aware of the restrictions placed upon them as women in a patriarchal society in which marriage is considered their true destiny. Being married is the only way to escape the unwanted sexual attention of the male sex, who regard single women pretty much as prey. Burney makes it clear at the end of

Cecilia, in which the heroine has been subjected to a great deal of unwanted male attention, just how pragmatic the decision to marry can be, and how it highlights the poverty of the choices that are available to women of the period. Given the conditions of her uncle's will, Cecilia, an orphan brought up by him, has to give up her sizeable inheritance if her husband refuses to take the family name – which neither he nor his father will countenance. Although she does decide to give it up, and feels sure of her husband's affection, she still feels a certain regret, and muses that although she has 'all the happiness human life seems capable of receiving: – yet human it was, and as such imperfect!'[47] She concludes her reflections by taking as positive a line on this as she can: 'Rationally, however, she surveyed the world at large, and finding that of the few who had any happiness, there were none without some misery, she checked the rising sigh of repining mortality, and, grateful with general felicity, bore partial evil with cheerfullest resignation.'[48] This is not an unconditional endorsement of the married state, nor of the human condition in general, where 'misery' will aways intrude at some point. In effect, this is marriage as the best of a bad lot, and that is at least a proto-feminist standpoint.

Separatist feminism is not the only cultural theory to be criticized as determinist. Marxism often is too, on the basis that it posits an underlying dialectic running through history which reveals itself as class struggle. We are essentially powerless to resist this dynamic, although we can take advantage of it to bring forward the end of class struggle in the 'dictatorship of the proletariat'. Marxists emphasize the factor of human agency in bringing this about, but in all interpretations of the theory seen to date, such as communism, the inevitability of certain events occurring does seem to become something of a mantra. A historical dialectic is just taken to be a fact of existence. Opponents regard this as a way of deflecting criticism, rather in the way that monotheistic religions do by claiming to be in sole possession of the 'truth'. Marxists consider their theory to be liberating and optimistic about humanity's future, but it does involve a refusal to listen to contrary viewpoints, which is to hold a pessimistic view about human nature as well as effectively excluding the factor of difference from human affairs.

Structuralism, too, has a deterministic bias in its notion of there being deep structures working within the many systems that constitute our world. Claude Lévi-Strauss claimed in *The Raw and the Cooked*, for example, that there was a common pattern to the creation myths of South American tribes, to the extent that they were to be regarded as 'transformations occurring within a set';[49] that is, variations of a source theme that was to be found throughout various cultures. At best, we were channels for those deep structures to work through: 'it is language which speaks, not the author', as Roland Barthes theorized the writing process, for example.[50] This would appear to reduce the importance of human agency quite drastically, since it is deep structures that are dictating our responses to events, much in the way that genetic determinists believe our genetic structure does. To claim that 'only language acts' is to curb the scope for free will very considerably.

What is questionable about all such determinist theories is that they involve a form of fundamentalism, insisting that the reality of the underlying structures they posit cannot be called into question. Individuals are seen to be under the control of impersonal forces: 'only language acts', and so forth.[51] There is little evidence of scepticism coming into play here; rather the theories are working from a basic set of beliefs that are taken to be beyond doubt. It is denialism in action yet again.

* * *

Reasons for pessimism do seem to keep being discovered, no matter how much optimists try to convince us that they no longer apply in our own time, and that the future is set fair to be 'magnificent'. Set fair for whom? And at whose cost? One person's ever-improving lifestyle is another's zero-hours contract misery, or exploitation by a Western multinational in the developing world. It needs to be pointed out, too, that if the worst is never certain to arrive, then neither is the best. Pessimism in reaction to the events and phenomena such as those considered in this chapter would seem to be eminently justifiable, an acknowledgement of just how serious life can frequently be and how much it can tax our powers.

THREE

Optimists v. Pessimists:
Economics and Politics

An unshakeable belief in continuing progress lies at the heart of most modern economic theory, very notably in what is regarded as the current economic paradigm: neo-liberalism. So engrained has the expectation of progress become among the general public after such a prolonged his-torical experience of progress in technological terms, leading to an ever-improving quality of life (in the West anyway), that we rarely question the principle or the theories that under-pin it. Any voices that do question it, greens or 'de-growth' theorists, for example, though they are listened to respectfully enough, do not express the sentiments of the majority.[1] An improving economy is taken to be the norm in our everyday lives. It is what all governments strive to deliver, knowing that their popularity depends upon it. Political parties that argue for the opposite, perhaps offering to implement policies for de-growth if elected, do not tend to win much support.

Neo-liberalist optimism about the beneficial effects of the free market – 'market fundamentalism', as it is also known – is apparently resistant to all evidence to the contrary. I am in profound disagreement with this position. To claim that the largely unexpected and unpredicted – by the majority of mainstream economists, anyway – credit crash of 2007–8 will be the last of its kind simply seems unrealistic to pessimists like myself. Cast even a cursory eye over economic history and you will soon note that booms and busts are not the exception but the general rule. This ought to encourage a certain degree of scepticism. For the economic historian Charles P. Kindleberger, modern economic history can best be described as a series of 'manias, panics, and crashes', as can be seen in such phenomena as the infamous South Sea Bubble of the early eighteenth century, or the wildly inflated market for tulip bulbs in seventeenth-century Holland.[2] In more recent times there was the equally infamous Great Depression of the 1930s, the product of the catastrophic collapse of the Wall Street market after the fevered trading of the Roaring Twenties, and the various depressions that punctuated the economic growth fuelled by industrialization in the nineteenth century, such as the Long Depression of the 1870s.

Yet despite the historical record, before the latest crash broke we were being earnestly assured by the neo-liberal community that such an event would probably never occur again – just as long as we adhered to their economic programme of a free market with minimal government interference or formal regulation. Market fundamentalism was to be the solution to all our economic problems. How wrong can you be? I think it is up to the pessimistic to say.

Michael Lewis's *Flash Boys* presents a particularly depressing account of how Wall Street has simply rolled on regardless since the latest credit crash, finding ways round even the few safeguards the government has felt compelled to introduce to monitor financial trading since then. These methods are often very devious and of suspect legality once you scrutinize them closely. As Lewis points out, there are few on the outside who really know how the stock market functions nowadays, and how much it has changed from the traditional perception of it as traders frantically making deals on a packed trading floor:

> Over the past decade, the financial markets have changed too rapidly for our mental picture of them to

remain true to life . . . The U.S. stock market now trades inside black boxes, in heavily guarded buildings in New Jersey and Chicago. What goes on inside those black boxes is hard to say.[3]

Governments seem just as much in the dark as the general public, which a pessimist would think we should find very worrying. So, it would appear, are most of the higher management of the banks and finance houses involved in trading – which is probably even more worrying. It has been alarming to observe how those at the top of this industry were blissfully unaware of the risks being taken by their employees until disaster struck (as in the notorious case of Lehman Brothers). In the forthright words of Serge Latouche, a noted critic of our obsessively growth-based economic policies: 'We are in a performance car that has no driver, no reverse gear and no brakes and it is going to slam into the limitations of the planet.'[4]

Lewis paints a picture of a toxic environment on Wall Street, where traders are engaged in a perpetual cut-throat struggle to gain advantage over their competitors: advantage for their own personal benefit rather than the customer's, that is. Social conscience is conspicuous by its absence in a field where there are huge fortunes to be made in a very short time. The 'flash boys' are in it for themselves only and are milking the system for all it is worth. There has been no substantial change in psychology to suggest that much improvement is likely to be forthcoming if the sector is left to its own devices, as it keeps arguing it should be; the 'flash boys' display a truly impressive ingenuity at deflecting the few attempts made at bringing about reform of the financial markets. Lewis traces the efforts of one such reform-minded movement from within the system over the course of the book, but as its initiator sums it up: 'We know how to cure this . . . It's just a matter of whether the patient wants to be treated.'[5] As far as the 'flash boys' are concerned, the answer is a resounding 'no'.

It is difficult not to respond pessimistically to what books like this are telling us. Lewis is just the latest in a line of authors to expose the inner workings of the financial system, but he goes into far more inside detail than most of the others, and the message that comes out loud and clear is that the stock market currently operates without reference to any moral code.[6] In blunt terms, 'it was rigged. The icon of global capitalism was a fraud.'[7] Greed flourishes without careful monitoring, and little account is taken of its effect on others. Pessimism is the necessary check we are well advised to place on human nature in such cases, and it leads us to expect the worst if we give human beings absolutely free rein. The chaotic world of Wall Street is proof enough of that maxim; freedom from one perspective can look like anarchy from another. In the jaundiced view of an insider of the American financial system, when it comes to the new breed of stock market traders, set free by the new generation of high-speed computer systems, some 'would sell their grand-mothers' in exchange for a microsecond's advantage over their competitors.[8]

In the aftermath of Lewis's exposé (and the many others like it), various American government bodies have made it clear that they too have been monitoring the practices of both banks and the new breed of 'high frequency traders', and that they are planning to take appropriate action against them in due course. One would have to be extremely optimistic to think that new legislation alone would curb abuses of the market, however, because those who profit from such abuses are indefatigable in finding loopholes in whatever legislation is put in place. If the credit crash of 2007–8 was not enough of a wake-up call to them of the risks they are taking at the public's expense, then what would be? The mindset has not really changed appreciably, and, predictably enough, Lewis's claim that the market is rigged has met with a storm of criticism from within the market community. The pessimist would expect no less of those who have structured their lives so firmly around greed and a 'get rich quick' philosophy.

The optimism expressed by neo-liberals that the free-market system is the way to a more prosperous future for all, guaranteeing a much higher quality of life, is by no means shared by all who are subject to it. Matt Ridley's claim about how it benefits the poor no less than the rich does not hold up all that well when it comes to the developing world, where a high proportion of the West's consumer goods are now made under licence. Globalization has proved to be a very mixed blessing there, enriching politicians and industrialists in those countries far more than it ever has those actually toiling away on the factory floor. Commentators such as Naomi Klein, in her book *No Logo*, have been scathing about the working conditions and wages that employees in manufacturing in the developing world have to endure.[9] It is a situation that is all the more scandalous when it involves the production of high-profile branded goods that make the multinationals in question huge profits when sold to Western consumers. Nike is a frequently mentioned case, with Apple also coming under fire in connection with the manufacture of its computers in China. As Klein and other critics point out, it is the multinationals that are the dominant partners in this arrangement, since they are free to move elsewhere in the search for ever-lower production costs. Countries can find themselves effectively held to ransom by the threat of withdrawal by a multinational, and if savings must be made then these will be at the expense of vulnerable factory workers, squeezing what little they receive in the 'trickle down' stakes. There always seems to be some other poor nation willing to undercut existing arrangements, no matter how low they may be, and the multinationals can play the rivals off against each other to their own advantage. In addition, medical care in such countries is not up to a Western standard, often being very primitive or all but non-existent in the more remote rural areas. However, we go on buying the products despite the conditions that prevail for their workers.

Even when we move to the West to consider what the impact of neo-liberal policies has been there, the evidence hardly supports the claim that the poor are even greater beneficiaries than the rich. The gap between rich and poor throughout the West has widened quite significantly in the last few decades, especially in those countries which have been most enthusiastic about neo-liberalism: the USA and Britain. Add to this the growing trend towards part-time and zero-hours employment contracts (a system whereby employees have no guaranteed hours of work, but must be available on an on-call basis if and when their employer demands their services), and a picture emerges of a culture where those at the bottom have little cause to view the future with much optimism. Instead, for an increasing proportion of people the far likelier outlook is one of long-term economic insecurity, minimal employment rights and rapidly dwindling career prospects, especially with the vigorous anti-union policies pursued by the larger corporate employers in the name of greater employment 'flexibility' (a word that should alert pessimists to be on the lookout for something suspect being promoted). The term 'the precariat' has been coined to describe this steadily growing group, and for them the promises of neo-liberalism can only seem hollow – a crude attempt to disguise the fact that for the majority the worst quite plainly looms on the horizon.

The precariat have a clear historical lineage: they are our own era's version of Marx's proletariat: those at the bottom of the socio-economic heap who are mercilessly exploited by ruthless employers. To be able to make such a comparison, to indicate that the system has been allowed to reproduce such an unfair, unjust class structure this long after Marx's monumental critique, has to stand as an indictment of that system. Guy Standing is one of the foremost chroniclers of this phenomenon in his books *The Precariat: The New Dangerous Class* and *A Precariat Charter: From Denizens to Citizens*.[10] Standing's main point is that this new (or should we say reborn?) class poses a problem for the neo-liberal consensus in that since they no longer have any real stake in their society, they cannot be depended upon to support that system indefinitely. The precariat are to be thought of as 'denizens' rather than 'citizens' and have a rapidly declining sense of loyalty towards their culture's institutions, which do not seem to have their interests at heart. Having become the recipients of what can only be termed a worst-case economic scenario, the precariat feel excluded from the apparent benefits of the free market, and their frustration could, and Standing thinks definitely should, make them dangerous to those in power. An optimist like Ridley would most likely consider this just so much empty left-wing rhetoric, but it is also a warning of the potentially adverse consequences of optimism being allowed to run riot. It is asking a lot of anyone to be a daring optimist on a zero-hours contract.

Whether the precariat prove to be as dangerous to the socio-economic order as Standing believes they could be is a more contentious issue. They may not develop the kind of class consciousness that Marx attributed to the proletariat, and the reality of that, as well as its revolutionary potential, has been much disputed by social historians. Even the noted Marxist philosopher Georg Lukács expressed reservations about the latter, observing in 1921, in the aftermath of the Russian Revolution, that 'the revolutionary experiences of recent years have demonstrated clearly the *limits of revolutionary spontaneity*', on the basis that proletarian class consciousness was not necessarily as homogenous an entity as orthodox Marxists had assumed.[11] What the masses need, in this reading, is the Communist Party to show it the way, which takes us into altogether more problematical territory. The precariat is an even more disparate group than the old working-class proletariat, with far less in common with each other, so Standing might well be overstating the case, interesting though his theory is.

The tendency of a neo-liberal economic programme to create a progressively wider division between the haves and the have-nots, substantially increasing the pool of have-nots in the process, has not escaped the attention of the noted French economist Thomas Piketty. His book *Capital in the Twenty-first Century* is a withering assessment of the prevailing economic system and its devastating impact on the social fabric of the West, and Piketty goes into considerable historical detail to assess the patterns of wealth accumulation and distribution in the West over the last few centuries. While he offers some guidelines as to how the system could be reformed, Piketty remains aware of how difficult it will be to put these into practice given the stranglehold that the 'haves' currently exert on economic policy, not just in the West but around the globe. It would be optimistic to the point of being unrealistic to hope that there could be an outbreak of social conscience among the real beneficiaries of the neo-liberal agenda – the rich – so efficient is it in delivering ever greater returns to its backers. Tracing the long-term trends that have led to the ascendancy of neo-liberal doctrine in economic affairs, Piketty notes that despite the claims made by capitalism's cheerleaders of its value to society, 'the deep structures of capital and inequality' identified by such social commentators as Marx in the nineteenth century have become even more solidly entrenched in recent years.[12] It is a trend which will be extremely difficult to arrest; the growing ranks of the precariat surely stand witness to that.

Piketty's study represents a plea for the return of political economy to replace the current mathematically based model, which is largely oblivious to the social context of the economy and has overturned the gains made over the course of the twentieth century, particularly since the Second World War, in narrowing the gap between rich and poor. We should be pessimistic about trusting to the goodwill of those running the markets to undertake any programme of reform voluntarily. Piketty counsels against entirely losing hope of the possibility of reform being introduced, and ultimately being successful no matter how much the major owners of capital oppose it, exhorting us to remember that: 'As always, the worst is never certain to arrive.'[13] The pessimist would agree with him, but with the qualification that experience would tell us that as long as we give human nature free rein in a wealth-obsessed culture like ours, then the worst is far more likely to arrive than not. The return of the proletariat in the guise of the precariat is thought-provoking in that respect.

The financial establishment has been just as critical of Piketty's claims as it has of Lewis's, with the *Financial Times* raising doubts about Piketty's statistics and thus the conclusions drawn from them. *The Economist* has argued that even if there are some gaps in Piketty's statistics (which he has made available online to other researchers for checking), that does not necessarily invalidate his conclusions. Battle lines are being drawn in the economics profession on essentially ideological grounds, which will come as no surprise to Piketty, who is well aware that he is calling into question the entire methodological approach of recent economics. To those of us on the left, such a challenge is absolutely necessary if we are to achieve any measure of social justice at all.

Neo-liberalism puts profit at the very centre of its ethos, pursuing it with an almost religious zeal. Almost anything can be justified if it makes a profit or, even better, increases profits. Globalization has proved to be a boon in increasing profit margins since it has opened up a pool of cheaper labour in the developing world, which raises all sorts of awkward moral issues that most multinationals simply ignore: profit takes precedence, especially when there are shareholders involved. It is now enshrined in company law that companies are under an obligation to maximize shareholder returns, and this tends to promote a blinkered attitude as to how profits are made – as well as encouraging even higher levels of greed. Playing the shareholder card is taken to trump all objections, as the 'godfather' of neo-liberal economics, the American economist Milton Friedman, fully intended it to:

> There is one and only one social responsibility of business – to use its resources and engage in activities designed to increase its profits so long as it stays within the rules of the game, which is to say, engages in open and free competition without deception or fraud.[14]

What seemed bluntly radical back in the 1960s, when Friedman was first voicing such ideas, is now simply taken to be received wisdom. Shareholders would consider themselves to be short-changed should companies act in any other way, and would soon make their displeasure known – perhaps even to the extent of taking legal action.

Consumers in the West benefit from the lower prices that globalization delivers, thus enabling them to keep more of the 'profits' of their own labours, so a blind eye is turned to how their clothes, food and technological items – computers, for example, the hardware for which is largely made in the developing world, such as China – are produced, the working practices they involve and so on. Neo-liberalism encourages greed throughout society, and although campaigns against the exploitation of the developing world do break out on occasion, they do not appear to have much lasting effect on the overall system.

The fact that most governments in the West embraced neo-liberalism, and have largely kept faith with it despite the credit crash, has done little for the reputation of politicians in general and in consequence has inspired new levels of pessimism about them as a class. The austerity programmes they have introduced do not appear to be having much, if any, effect on the 'haves'. The ex-foreign correspondent of *The Times* newspaper Louis Heren, as quoted by the television interviewer Jeremy Paxman, is supposed to have encapsulated how he often felt when speaking to politicians: 'Why is this lying bastard lying to me?'[15] This attitude may never have been more succinctly put. It may be carrying it a bit far to claim that nothing a politician says can ever be taken on trust, but maintaining a certain degree of pessimism with regard to politicians is surely no bad thing. Democracies probably could not exist without it. Pessimism about the stock market, however, and a truly deep pessimism at that, should be taken as a given: there, exponential increases in trading speed are generating exponential increases in greed.

I am not suggesting that we sink into gloom over this dominance of greed in the financial world, or that pessimists would think that any action taken to curb this trait is pointless. Rather I think that we should acknowledge the dangers of this aspect of our nature, which is stronger in some than others, being allowed to run riot. Pessimism is about doing everything we can to check our meaner, self-interested side from coming to the fore, because we know that it will if it is allowed to. But it is a long, tough struggle that requires constant vigilance. Fatalists would probably shrug their shoulders and turn away; pessimists would sigh, then get on with the task nevertheless.

You cannot really detach economics from politics, of course, and the fetish for neo-liberalism does raise questions about the judgement of our political class. Postmodern theory insists that there has been a reaction against authoritarian belief systems in our time (more on this in chapter Four), and it is noticeable that the reputation of politicians has gone down fairly sharply of late. The level of respect they usually received in previous times is no longer there. Political promises are invariably treated with scepticism by a significant proportion of the electorate in most Western countries, who are only too aware of how often these have been broken in the past, as well as of the limitations that politicians are subject to in trying to implement any promises they may have made in order to get elected in the first place. Many of us now assume that it is likely that circumstances will conspire against any truly determined attempt at reform of, say, the financial world, as various political parties admit is necessary and even advance policies for. But policies are not practice, and we have been disappointed regularly on this score in recent years (let us hope we will not always be so). Neo-liberalism just has too firm a grip on the markets these days, and the major players have the power to block or curtail government policies in their area.

The growing feeling that politicians cannot be trusted suggests there is a lot more pessimism around among the public than might be thought, and that the optimism preached by the Ridleys of our time might be a harder sell than they have assumed. The precariat, for one, is going to be very difficult to convince of how marvellous life is steadily becoming in the twenty-first century; for them, it mainly seems to mean growing insecurity. Unemployment is a huge social problem throughout Western Europe, with no obvious solution on the horizon, so why should political promises be believed any more? Falling turnouts at general elections throughout most of the West might be taken to indicate that many are not even bothering to take notice of those promises.

Another community where pessimism about politics and politicians is rife is in the African American population of America – the first African American President in the nation's history notwithstanding. The majority of the political class in America is white, as is the majority of the population, and the African American community justifiably feels that it has not benefitted from the country's wealth as much as their white counterparts have; that the system is weighted against them.

With average earnings significantly lower, as well as levels of educational attainment, poverty is much more widespread among African Americans than whites; the former group's living conditions are in general markedly worse too, with all the attendant problems this brings, such as drugs and crime. The economic downturn since the credit crash has affected those at the lower end of the social scale far more than it has those at the top, and the African American community has inevitably felt this particularly keenly. Race relations are better than they used to be, and substantial progress has been made in this area since the middle of the last century, but discrimination still exists and is bitterly resented in the African American community.

Politicians may go on about America being the land of opportunity, but it may not seem that way from an African American perspective; pessimism about the reality of such claims is an entirely understandable reaction. Piketty's book provides chapter and verse on how the scope for opportunity has dwindled for those outside the elite, who are the owners of capital; how in fact there is no longer a level playing field for rich and poor, but one in which economic inequality is steadily widening across the social scale. He fears that if we go on in the same way, the discrepancy between rich and poor will revert to that experienced in the nineteenth century (the heyday of laissez-faire capitalism), with wealth accumulation increasing ever faster for those at the top at the expense of the bulk of the country's population. Living in an African American ghetto might well make you feel that you were right at the sharp end of this process.

The rise of right-wing populism in America in recent years, with its predominantly white appeal (the Tea Party movement being a case in point), is not calculated to make the African American community feel any more sanguine about its prospects. Both the Tea Party and the Republican Party are committed to reducing government spending as much as they can (although defence spending usually seems to escape the worst of this when in Republican hands), and such cuts disproportionately hit the poorer sections of the population, who are more likely to access government-funded welfare programmes. Again, this is not in the interests of the African American population, who have a far greater dependence on these. 'ObamaCare', for example, benefits those at the lower end of the socio-economic scale most of all, but one would be hard pressed to be optimistic about the future of government-funded healthcare in America, which will most likely struggle to survive any future Republican administration. A newly elected Republican senator, Joni Ernst, screened a television ad during the election campaign of herself at target practice on a firing range, complete with a voiceover saying, 'Once she sets her sight on ObamaCare, Joni's gonna unload.'[16]

Pessimism would be the appropriate reaction, too, when it comes to assessing what the emergence of the Tea Party says about human nature, with their belief that the only thing wrong with their country is government itself, and their opposition to almost any kind of public spending at all (wasting their hard-earned money on others, as they conceive of it). The notion that everything will work out all right if we remove all controls on human beings and leave them completely free of any official interference is optimism taken to the extreme. In this instance it seems based on a romantic vision of pioneer life on the frontier, when central government was barely in evidence much of the time, and settlers could simply go ahead and do what they felt was right; the native population, of course, saw things very differently. The left is often identified with 'big' government and its tendency to interfere in almost all aspects of human affairs (the worst example of it being the Soviet 'command economy'), and that concept certainly can be criticized. While agreeing that an authoritarian style of government is not in the wider public interest, I think we ought to be very wary of trusting to the better side of our natures and having none at all.

Being on the left these days does, however, give one reasons aplenty to be pessimistic about the way politics is going. Socialism in various forms was a significant factor in twentieth-century socio-political life, but it has hit hard times in the twenty-first. The collapse of the Soviet project and the introduction of capitalist methods into the communist Chinese economy are but the most obvious signs of this decline, and only the most diehard of Marxists will bemoan this. Still, it has been symptomatic of a marked shift away from socialist ideals towards a more middle-ground, social-democratic position that has made its peace with market economics, going along with the widely touted notion that the globalized free market was 'the only game in town'. To some of us, politics has shifted further than we would have wanted in this direction. New Labour followed that route only to be blamed by its opponents, and then the electorate at large, for the credit crash that brought the neo-liberal boom period (or, more correctly, bubble) to an end. Trust in the market was severely misplaced in this instance, and the irony was only too apparent. There is every reason to be sceptical about continuing in this vein, as neo-liberals are urging us to do, and that is one of the major sources of my own pessimism. Expect more manias, panics and crashes – as well as a growing precariat, as companies exploit the situations these create.

FOUR

I Think, Therefore I Expect the Worst: Pessimism in Philosophy

Almost any topic or aspect of life and the world we live in can become a subject of philosophical attention: 'life, the universe, and everything' well describes the range of the discipline's interests. Philosophers can, and do, deal with the very smallest and the very largest of issues, from whether our arguments are well-constructed and unambiguous in meaning in everyday discourse, to what our place in the universal scheme of things is – indeed, whether there *is* a universal scheme of things at all. Philosophical thought often generates uncomfortable conclusions. At the beginnings of modern philosophy, René Descartes put forward his famous principle of *cogito ergo sum*, 'I think, therefore I am', arguing that 'this proposition "I am", "I exist", whenever I utter it or conceive it in my mind, is necessarily true.'[1] But other than a thinking being, exactly *what* am I? And can I assume the trustworthiness of my thinking process? The nature of personal identity is a problem that has taxed modern philosophers very considerably, and continues to do so right through to our own day. Not everyone in the field has been as sanguine as Descartes that they have managed to resolve it once and for all. Wrestling with such problems inevitably brings philosophers up against the limitations of our understanding and experience, and pessimism about the human condition can very often follow closely behind.

Arguments about the limitations of our understanding and experience are not confined to modern philosophy, however, and can be found back in the earliest days of Western philosophy in Greek classical times. Scepticism was a movement which developed out of that tradition, challenging many of its founding assumptions, and I shall be regarding it as an ally in the fight against optimism. Sceptics raised awkward questions about the nature of truth and proof, casting doubt on the reliability of our knowledge. These doubts have continued to haunt philosophical discourse ever since. Some of the most important, and controversial, movements in recent philosophy, such as poststructuralism and postmodernism, have based themselves heavily on scepticism, embracing a particularly radical form of it that their opponents tend to find very disorienting.

Scepticism arose as a philosophical position in classical Greece in relation to establishing theories of knowledge (the branch of philosophy known as epistemology). It became apparent that all philosophical theories depended upon a starting point that was assumed to be true beyond any reasonable doubt. With that building block in place, you could construct quite elaborate theories. There were basic laws of logic that everyone just had to accept, such as the law of identity: that a thing was identical to itself – in other words, that it was a truth that a thing was identical to itself. (Whether the law of identity actually holds has become one of the most contentious topics of modern philosophy.) Certain thinkers in ancient Greece, such as the Pyrrhonian school, started to question these basic laws, pointing out that it was no more than an assumption that the starting point was true, and that theories of truth had to be based on something provable. That required yet another starting point, but what proved that one true? And so on in an infinite regress. The upshot was that we could never really know anything with certainty.

You can easily tie yourself in knots with such ways of thinking, and philosophers have had to devise various ways of sidestepping scepticism in order to theorize at all. Religious philosophy has particular problems with scepticism because its starting point is that God (or whatever divinity applies to a particular tradition) actually exists. Cast that into doubt, and religion itself has no basis at all: everything else is predicated on it. Again, various ways round this have been developed, but to a sceptic these can never be totally convincing. For sceptics the only question that needs to be asked of any believer is 'What proves the existence of God?', and there will never be a foolproof answer to this. Ultimately belief in the existence of God is a matter of faith, not logical reasoning – not that this has stopped generations of Christian philosophers from trying.

Pyrrhonian scepticism has come down to us through the work of Sextus Empiricus, and his third-century AD work *Outlines of Scepticism*, which codified the ideas originally developed by the movement's founder, Pyrrho of Elis, a somewhat shadowy figure of the fourth to third century BC who left no extant writings. Pyrrhonism's major target was dogmatism: it argued that we could never reach a state of absolute certainty about what we knew. All we were left with, therefore, was beliefs which we could not prove were true, there being no 'agreed standard' by which we could reach such a decision – only the misguided assumption of one.[2] Dogmatic insistence on the truth of your beliefs was to Sextus an untenable position. The point of Pyrrhonian scepticism was to make apparent 'the conceit and rashness of the Dogmatists' so that others could avoid such errors of judgement.[3] Pyrrhonism went so far as to cast doubt on the validity of beliefs in general, a sweeping claim with far-reaching implications for the way we live. As far as Sextus Empiricus was concerned, 'to every account an equal account is opposed; for it is from this, we think, that we come to hold no belief.'[4]

Scepticism is, therefore, an essentially negative position to adopt, and at the very least that can induce feelings of unease in those who come across it. Holding no beliefs at all will strike most people, especially non-philosophers, as unnatural and inconsistent with social existence, which would be unthinkable without some sort of a belief system behind it. Religion and politics, for example, would lose most of their point if we could not believe anything at all that their leaders said (although some cynics might say that we rarely could anyway, particularly when it came to politicians). Sceptics, on the other hand, have traditionally relished demolishing the foundations of belief systems, even if they cannot offer any viable alternatives to them. Taken to its logical conclusion, scepticism leaves one in limbo.

Although it declined in importance during the ensuing Christian period in European history, Pyrrhonism was later to be revived in the sixteenth century through the work of such figures as the essayist Michel de Montaigne, and its rejection of dogmatism resonates throughout scepticism in modern times. To its detractors, however, such a theory could easily generate a sense of pessimism in others with its insistence on there being no 'agreed standard' by which we reach the truth of anything, or have any certain knowledge whatsoever. We would have nothing more substantial than a relative notion of truth to go by, hardly the most suitable of bases on which to ground, for example, moral codes – and then the laws subsequently devised to ensure that these are upheld. When it comes to our own time, poststructuralists and postmodernists have subjected the notion of an 'agreed standard' to an even more sustained attack than the Pyrrhonists did, and have undermined the validity of belief systems with even greater relish.

Arguably the most important sceptic of modern times is the eighteenth-century philosopher David Hume, who managed to problematize one of the most basic assumptions of science by arguing that there was no necessary connection between cause and effect. As far as Hume was concerned, there was no more than a probability that a given cause would have the same effect as it had done before, because we had nothing more concrete to go on than previous experience, or 'custom', as he referred to it: 'after the constant conjunction of two objects – heat and flame, for instance, weight and solidity – we are determined by custom alone to expect the one from the appearance of the other.'[5] That was no guarantee that the same cause and effect would occur in the future, so the next time around something entirely unexpected might happen. Just because the sun has risen every day in the past in human history does not constitute proof that it will again tomorrow. As Ludwig Wittgenstein put it in the twentieth century: 'It is an hypothesis that the sun will rise tomorrow: and this means that we do not *know* whether it will rise.'[6] We have no knowledge of the future, in other words, only a probable belief based on past experience; so while we can plan for the future, we cannot ensure that those plans will work out as experience tells us they should.

Hume's philosophical work could, he admitted, leave him feeling insecure, and it does appear to undermine some of our most basic assumptions about the world and how it works. His solution was to immerse himself in the pleasures of everyday life, but that is not of course a philosophical solution to the problem, which does seem to render certain knowledge about anything all but impossible. For an epistemologist that really is the worst-case scenario.

Thomas Hobbes is a philosopher with an extremely pessimistic attitude towards human nature. Hobbes's *Leviathan* argues that all human beings are motivated in the first instance by an instinct for survival that will lead us to act purely out of self-interest without any real regard for others: the Hobbesian 'natural man' is not much of a social being. We cannot help acting that way:

> The right of nature . . . is the Liberty each man hath, to use his own power, as he will himselfe, for the

preservation of his own Nature; that is to say, of his own
Life; and consequently, of doing any thing, which in his
own Judgement, and Reason, hee shall conceive to be
the aptest means thereunto.[7]

This is life in the 'state of nature', before organized societies
come onto the scene to constrain individuals in the name of
public order. In Hobbes's memorable phrase, the condition is
'nasty, brutish, and short', with individuals effectively in a permanent state of war with their fellows, given that each of them
is struggling to exercise their power on their own behalf by
what they perceive 'to be the aptest means'.[8] (It has to be said,
however, that since this 'state' is supposed to have existed
before recorded history, there is an element of imaginative
projection going on here.) Everyone is therefore everyone
else's enemy, which means there is no sense of long-term
security for anyone, no matter how physically strong and
resourceful they may be. Even the strongest can be caught out
in an unguarded moment.

The drastic solution put forward by Hobbes was a society
in which absolute power was invested in one individual
(following on from the practice of the time, a monarch,
although a dictator would do just as well), with individuals
having no rights at all against this power's sovereign decisions:
'nothing the Soveraign Representative can doe to a Subject,
on what pretence soever, can properly be called Injustice, or
Injury'.[9] In return for giving away their rights, the absolute
sovereign agrees to guarantee security for all those under his
or her power. From a twenty-first century perspective this
looks much like a police state, but to Hobbes, who had lived
through the English Civil War of the 1640s, it was the only
way to rein in humanity's natural instincts, which ran riot
when absolute sovereignty was removed. (There are some
parallels to be noted here with Machiavelli, who had earlier
put the case for an absolute ruler as the best way to ensure an

ordered polity in *The Prince*.[10]) This was what Hobbes believed had happened in 1640s England with the challenge to royal power by Parliament and the ensuing hostilities, which ended in the execution of the reigning monarch, Charles I, and the establishment of a republic in 1649. It represented a resolutely pessimistic assessment of human nature on Hobbes's part, as something which could not change for the better, but could only be tamed by a greater force. This is a viewpoint which can find support even today. Dictatorships still exist, as do ruthless oligarchies, and they usually try to justify themselves by claiming to be the only bulwark against chaos.

An argument for the need to have an authoritarian bulwark against chaos can be found right back at the very beginnings of Western philosophy, in Plato. His major work *The Republic* envisages a severely hierarchical society as the best way to maintain public order. Plato was very aware that his native Athens had suffered from much political turmoil in the later fifth century BC, with democracy lapsing for a while under the rule of the oligarchic Thirty Tyrants. The ideal society, Plato maintained, would consist of three classes: guardians, auxiliaries and the general public respectively. Each class had a clearly delineated role within the polity: guardians ruled; auxiliaries acted as a combination of army and police force to enforce the guardians' orders; and the general public carried out the many practical activities (trades and services, and so on) the society required to be provided to continue on an everyday basis. Authority rested solely with the guardians, and this was the way to avoid internal conflict and political dissension, according to Plato. Without such a system there was the constant threat of a class war breaking out between the rich and the poor, and a consequent decline into civil disorder. In Plato's view, democracy was not the way to prevent this.

Plato conceived of ruling as an art, and the guardians were to be educated to prepare them properly for their duties in exercising this. As rulers, they were expected always to have the interests of the state at heart, and one of their key roles was to act as censors of the narratives that any citizens would be allowed to read, hear or see performed. This is one of the most contentious ideas floated in *The Republic*, and it rather interestingly prefigures Soviet socialist realism in the specifications laid down, as well as the justification for instituting them. Poets and dramatists are instructed to produce what is in effect propaganda that says only good things about the state and its rulers, and expresses no contrary opinions at all to the dominant ideology – including criticism of its religious beliefs: 'If a poet writes of the gods in this way, we shall be angry and refuse him the means to produce his play.'[11] Plato is even willing to go to the lengths of banishing any poet who does not follow the state's prescriptions: 'we shall tell him that we are not allowed to have any such person in our commonwealth . . . and conduct him to the borders of some other country'.[12] The Soviet system had no more patience with criticism, hence the development of socialist realism, with its strict rules about what creative artists were allowed to say or do.

Plato recognizes that poets have the ability to sway people's emotions, and if they are being critical of the dominant ideology, that could undermine people's faith in, and obedience to, their rulers. He thinks that most of us are too easily led by our emotions, and that steps therefore have to be taken to keep these in check: 'For our own benefit, we shall employ the poets and story-tellers of the more austere and less attractive type, who will . . . conform to those rules we laid down.'[13] In other words, human nature cannot really be trusted if left to its own devices. Hobbes was to reach the same conclusion, although his solution is even more totalitarian in style than Plato's.

Arthur Schopenhauer's vision of existence is desperately bleak, suggesting that the only way we can cope with its many trials and tribulations is to adopt an attitude of resolute asceticism: to expect the worst, because that is what awaits us sooner or later. He really does seem to be a case of 'I think, therefore I expect the worst', since he comes to the conclusion that there is ultimately nothing much to hope for out of life. Death is our unavoidable destination, and it will not be too much fun on the way there. As he solemnly warns us in his only too aptly titled essay 'On the Suffering of the World':

> If the immediate and direct purpose of life is not suffering then our existence is the most ill-adapted to its purpose in the world . . . Each individual misfortune, to be sure, seems an exceptional occurrence; but misfortune in general is the rule . . . Work, worry, toil and trouble are indeed the lot of almost all men their whole life long.[14]

He goes on in the same unsparing, comfortless fashion: 'Nonetheless, everyone desires to achieve old age, that is to say a condition in which one can say: "Today it is bad, and day by day it will get worse – until at last the worst of all arrives."'[15] The best he can find to say about our doomed journey through life is that at least as children we are unaware of the fate that is lined up for us ahead. Existence is simply a burden to be borne, with little pleasure to break up the dreary sequence.

Schopenhauer's other essays explore topics like 'On the Vanity of Existence': 'We shall do best to think of life as a *desengano*, as a process of disillusionment: since this is, clearly enough, what everything that happens to us is calculated to produce.'[16] Then there is 'On Suicide', which argues against the contemporary view of it as a crime: 'there is nothing in the world a man has a more incontestable *right* to than his own life and person.'[17] However, as Schopenhauer concedes, most of us do opt for old age instead despite what this will involve, as he did himself, surviving into his seventies. Suffering, pain and disillusionment are to him are what life primarily consists of. Understandable though suicide is under those circumstances, he is not recommending it: as Joshua Foa Dienstag notes, Schopenhauer will neither 'endorse' nor 'abhor' the act.[18]

It was the publication of essays such as these in the collection entitled *Parerga and Paralipomena* in 1851 that established Schopenhauer's reputation throughout Europe, and the ideas in them were to be much discussed in European intellectual circles over the rest of the century. Reading them now, some of these ideas leave a lot to be desired, however, such as those in his notorious essay 'On Women', which displays a misogynistic streak in the author's character. We are informed that women are 'not intended for great mental or for great physical labour', and that they are to be thought of as 'childish, silly and short-sighted, in a word big children'.[19] Views like these were not uncommon at the time, but they are still worth noting if we are trying to understand why biological essentialism could gain a foothold in the feminist movement – and then give rise to notions of separatism.

Schopenhauer's position has been called philosophical pessimism, and it has some heavyweight philosophical work behind it, mainly in the form of his major opus, *The World as Will and Idea* (*Idea* sometimes being translated as *Representation*). It begins with the assertion that 'The world is my idea', taking that to be 'a truth which holds good for everything that lives and knows'.[20] But there is a higher 'truth' we must recognize, and its ramifications are what the rest of this long and extremely dense work is designed to explore: 'This truth, which must be very serious and impressive if not awful to every one, is that a man can also say and must say, "the world is my will."'[21] While admiring the philosophy of the Stoics to some extent, Schopenhauer does not think it is possible to inure oneself to suffering and pain as Stoicism instructs us to do. Suffering remains an inescapable element of human existence and we must all experience it; a sentiment that Schopenhauer feels does come through in Indian philosophy, a very important influence on his thought. In consequence, our lives become largely a matter of suffering through repeated episodes of 'work, worry, toil and trouble' until we finally arrive at the dreaded 'worst of all'. The 'Will' demands that we recognize this brute fact, expecting us to structure our lives around it: 'freedom from all aim, from all limits, belongs to the nature of the will, which is an endless striving' (this aspect of his thought is often considered to pre-figure Sigmund Freud on the subconscious and its drives).[22] Even if we achieve what we are striving for at any one point in our lives, however, any satisfaction we experience will not last, and we shall find ourselves returning to the treadmill of 'endless striving'.[23] As far as Schopenhauer is concerned, 'We are fortunate enough if there still remains something to wish for and to strive after' – presumably also including old age, though a desperate condition that undoubtedly is.[24] This is not light reading by any means.

The last part of volume I of *The World as Will and Idea* makes the case that asceticism, based on the model of it found in Indian philosophy, is the only method by which one may overcome the life of misery that the Will imposes on us – although this will not remove suffering from our lives, merely our attitude towards it. We will still be aware of all the suffering being experienced in the world around us by our fellow human beings, but we will recognize what causes it and will not fall into the trap of thinking there is anything much we can do about it: it is just the human condition. How per-suasive we find this argument, however, or how practical, is up for debate. It does go against the grain of the way social existence is set up, plus the psychological make-up of the majority of us. Schopenhauer's description of the life that the Will will condemn us to if we do not opt for asceticism – and he does go on about misery, suffering, pain and sorrow at some considerable length – is what is likely to stick in most readers' minds after working their way through *The World as Will and Idea*, especially if they cannot quite bring themselves to embark on a life of asceticism. It is worth noting, however, that Schopenhauer himself did not lead a particularly ascetic existence.

The other volumes of the work are supplementary to volume I, expanding on the topics of its various sections, hammering the message home about just how painful life unavoidably is and insisting that optimism must be rejected: 'To this world it has been sought to apply the system of optimism, and demonstrate to us that it is the best of all possible worlds [as Leibniz had argued]. The absurdity is glaring.'[25] Schopenhauer pictures us as being more or less condemned by both nature and nurture, asserting that 'the will . . . constitutes the inner, true, and indestructible nature of man; in itself, however, it is unconscious', a notion which very much prefigures Freud, as the Will restlessly drives us on from desire to desire.[26] Nurture can offer us no relief, and we find ourselves caught in a double bind:

> Life with its hourly, daily, weekly, yearly, little, greater, and great misfortunes, with its deluded hopes and its accidents destroying all our calculations, bears so distinctly the impression of something with which we must become disgusted, that it is hard to conceive how one has been able to mistake this and allow oneself to be persuaded that life is there in order to be thankfully enjoyed, and that man exists in order to be happy.[27]

This passage seems to sum up the point of Schopenhauer's entire philosophical enterprise. What he is effectively saying is: 'Abandon hope, all ye who are born.'

At least one commentator argues that the complex and imposing edifice constructed in *The World as Will and Idea* is designed mainly to provide a basis for Schopenhauer's inveterate pessimism, and that does appear to be his principal legacy to intellectual debate. As R. J. Hollingdale puts it: 'There have been great pessimists before . . . but there has been none who tried with so great a show of learning to demonstrate that the pessimistic outlook is *justified*, that life itself really is bad.'[28] I do not think we need to carry pessimism to quite such an extreme as this (it can begin to verge on fatalism if we are not careful), but there is no denying the powerful impact that Schopenhauer's outlook has had. He is not someone to make you feel better about life, the universe and everything, and although I do think we have cause to oppose optimism, I would not agree that we have to go this far. Schopenhauer is never less than thought-provoking, however, and we can all experience that sinking feeling at times when thinking about the amount of 'work, worry, toil and trouble' that may well lie ahead of us – even if we know that that is not the whole story of what life is.

Friedrich Nietzsche is another nineteenth-century philosopher whose work is considered to be pessimistic in orientation, for all that he takes this in a different direction to Schopenhauer. Nietzsche's philosophy can be tricky to pin down, and has provided inspiration to movements as diverse as Nazism, poststructuralism and postmodernism. (Nazism found the notion of the 'overhuman', sometimes translated as 'superman', as outlined in *Thus Spoke Zarathustra*, very congenial to its racist purposes: '*I teach to you the Overhuman. The human is something that shall be overcome . . . All beings so far have created something beyond themselves.*'[29]) In ideological terms, that is a range going from fascism to anti-fascism. If there is one idea that is associated with Nietzsche more than any other, however, it is the 'death of God', which posits a post-religious universe in which we can draw no optimism from organized religion (scant though this admittedly could be in theologies like Calvinism).[30]

The 'death of God' throws our system of moral values into chaos, since we can no longer rely on religion to provide the basis for them (such as the Ten Commandments, for example), leaving us yet again with no 'agreed standard' against which they can be judged. Hence Nietzsche's insistence that 'we stand in need of a *critique* of moral values, *the value of these values itself should first of all be called into question*'.[31] Nietzsche is often seen as conducting a campaign against the tradition of rationalism in Western culture, making his work attractive to succeeding generations of like-minded thinkers, even if the conclusions Nietzsche reached from his campaign, such as the need for the development of 'overhumans' who would transcend the existing system of moral values, have proved considerably more contentious. Overall, Nietzsche displays a fairly pessimistic assessment of world culture and history.

In line with his appeal for a 'radical transvaluation' of contemporary values, Nietzsche also took an iconoclastic stance towards the concept of truth, arguing that there was no 'agreed standard' for this either:[32]

What, then, is truth? A mobile army of metaphors, metonymies, anthropomorphisms, in short a sum of human relations which have been subjected to poetic and rhetorical intensification, translation, and decoration, and which, after they have been in use for a long time, strike a people as firmly established, canonical, and binding; truths are illusions of which we have forgotten that they are illusions.[33]

It is this aspect of his work which has appealed most to poststructuralists and postmodernists, who espouse a similarly relativistic attitude to truth. Their claim is that in the absence of absolute truth, or any reliable method of determining this, authority should lose its power over us. If it cannot prove what it is saying, then why should we allow ourselves to be led by it and obey its dictates? Like Nietzsche, these latter-day schools of philosophy tend to treat the concept of truth as an illusion used by self-interested parties to exercise control over our thoughts and actions. It is intriguing to note that Nietzsche's theories could be put to such different uses by fascist and anti-fascist thinkers, because the former were very much obsessed with exercising control over the general public.

Theodor W. Adorno might be seen as a latter-day example of a philosophical pessimist, given his trenchant views on the trajectory of twentieth-century European culture. Adorno was highly critical of the political systems that had developed in his time, above all the fascism that had turned him into a refugee from Nazi Germany in the 1930s, along with many of his colleagues in the Institute for Social Research, which became known as the Frankfurt School, which relocated eventually to New York. Despite the alliance the two power blocs formed in the Second World War's fight against fascism, Adorno was also dismissive of both Soviet communism and Western democracy, developing an intense dislike for the mass culture propagated throughout the latter, which to him merely trivialized human experience. Looking around him, Adorno found a world bereft of mass political movements that could merit his unqualified support.

Writing with his Frankfurt School associate Max Horkheimer during the Second World War, the two voiced decidedly pessimistic sentiments about the legacy of the Enlightenment. Whereas this phenomenon was usually held to have promoted a new climate of reason in European culture that was instrumental in creating the modern world, and crucially the modern democratic nation state, Adorno and Horkheimer begged to differ: 'In the most general sense of progressive thought, the Enlightenment has always aimed at liberating men from fear and establishing their sovereignty. Yet the fully enlightened earth radiates disaster triumphant.'[34] Clearly, progressive thought is not felt by these thinkers to justify an optimistic worldview, and reason itself is something to be treated with a large dose of scepticism (the influence of

Nietzsche can be detected at such points – yet another indication of just how wide a range of positions his ideas could sustain). Adorno was, in his later career, to dismiss Marxism's claim even to be considered progressive, arguing in *Negative Dialectics* that it was based on false assumptions, particularly a misunderstanding about the nature of dialectics, which did not fall into the neat pattern that Marx had claimed, or reach an end that fitted his goals.[35] Adorno's interpretation was that the dialectic went on yielding contradictions, its open-endedness severely problematizing Marxist thought and the politics it had given rise to: the Marxist utopia just kept receding into the distance.

Adorno could identify little of merit in the modern world (no doubt he would have been even more appalled at the far more pervasive mass culture of the current day), and his philosophical writings can come across as one long complaint about its multiple failings, as well as about humankind's apparent ability to embrace these quite willingly. Humankind seemed only too gullible, only too willing to be led, either by unscrupulous politicians and theorists or corporate interests, and Adorno was pessimistic about any possibility of significant improvement on this score. He really did believe that, as far as our culture in general was concerned, the worst had happened, and he was reduced to being a Cassandra-like observer on the sidelines bemoaning the fact of its precipitate decline. One can just imagine how he would have reacted to such phenomena as Facebook and Twitter, not to mention 'reality' television. The older you get, the more you can fall into this style of 'grumpy old man' pessimism, but I do feel you should resist the temptation. Adorno sounds perilously close to suggesting that the situation is hopeless on occasion (much as Schopenhauer does), and that is not helpful to the development of a positive pessimism. I can well understand, however, how his experience as a refugee from Nazism could sour his outlook.

Jean-Paul Sartre's existentialism can sound close to Schopenhauer's version of pessimism in many ways, and there is a similar sense in his work of wanting us to face up to the less palatable aspects of human existence. *Being and Nothingness* pictures us as being 'abandoned' into existence in a world that has no intrinsic meaning.[36] It is an absurd situation to be placed in, and we would be foolish to pretend otherwise. Yet unfortunately this is what the bulk of humanity does most of the time, refusing to acknowledge the alienation that is an integral part of being human, and not willing to experience the anxiety that comes in its wake. To live an 'authentic' existence would be to recognize our alienated status rather than to hide from it, and Sartre spells out what this means for us as individuals in uncompromising terms: 'In anguish I apprehend myself at once as totally free and as not being able to derive the meaning of the world except as coming from myself.'[37] We cannot legitimately adopt any belief system, whether a political ideology or a religion (this is manifestly a world where 'God is dead'), to make good that deficiency: it really is down to us alone as isolated individuals, which places a considerable responsibility on our shoulders. The protagonist of Sartre's best-known novel, *Nausea*, Antoine Roquentin, shows just how difficult this can make our lives:

> If I am not mistaken, and if all the signs which are piling up are indications of a fresh upheaval in my life, well then, I am frightened. It isn't that my life is rich or weighty or precious, but I'm afraid of what is going to be born and take hold of me and carry me off – I wonder where?[38]

What takes hold of him is repeated attacks of 'nausea' that overwhelm him:

Things are bad! Things are very bad: I've got it, that filthy thing, the Nausea. And this time it's new: it caught me in a café . . . I can feel it *over there* on the wall, on the braces, everywhere around me. It is one with the café, it is I who am inside *it*.[39]

To shy away from the admittedly harsh reality of a life of anguish, on the other hand, is to be guilty of 'bad faith', and that is a cardinal sin in the existentialist universe.[40] As an example of living in bad faith, Sartre cites the case of a café waiter whose duties require him to subsume his own personality to the demands of his customers. When that happens, the waiter can no longer be said to be living for himself, but rather for others; as Sartre puts it, 'he is playing at being a waiter in a café'.[41] By performing a role with a routine set of activities he may be keeping anxiety at bay, but at the cost of denying his own freedom, failing to create a meaningful existence for himself in the world. Anyone else could step into his role at a moment's notice. There is nothing unique to him about it, just a series of repetitive tasks to be undertaken in the service of others. Religions have much the same effect of offering pre-planned roles to believers, promising an afterlife plus a specific role for humanity in a divine master plan. This constitutes a seductive alternative to a life full of anxiety.

Sartre envisages human existence as playing out against a background of 'nothingness', an entity that is lying in wait for us at any given moment in our lives, ready to cut off our efforts to be authentic individuals, 'coiled in the heart of being – like a worm'.[42] Even though we know that nothingness eventually must win, death being the inevitable climax of every human life, we must never surrender to it. Suicide therefore would be the ultimate act of bad faith. One can easily see why this would be found depressing by many readers: if there is no meaning to human life, and no God or higher force to provide one, then what is the point of it all? Especially if authentic existence means being permanently prey to anxiety, and we can never hope to overcome our feelings of alienation. Existentialism emphasizes just how alone we are as individuals, and that can be a terrifying prospect to most people (Calvinist predestination can work in much the same way, as we saw with John Bunyan). Sartre's argument is that as long as we are alive, we have at least the chance to create new meaning for our lives through the authenticity of our actions – and that does point towards a more positive form of pessimism than we can derive from Schopenhauer. Suicide would leave us at the mercy of the opinions of others, since 'at the moment of death we *are*; that is, we are defenceless before the judgments of others. They can decide *in truth* what we are.'[43]

So there is a point to going on after all, even if we know that 'the worst of all' cannot be avoided indefinitely; merely continuing on as, say, a café waiter would not count, of course. Pessimists can appreciate the underlying logic of the argument, as well as the condition of anguish that 'authentic' existence requires of us.

Albert Camus's essay *The Myth of Sisyphus*, which treats the fate of that Greek mythological character as symbolic of the sheer meaninglessness of human existence, provides a vivid illustration of the existentialist worldview. Condemned by the gods to push a heavy boulder up a steep hill, despite never quite managing to reach the top before it rolls back down, Sisyphus is left with no option but to return to the task each time around. Camus argues, however, that there is a certain degree of heroism to be detected in what Sisyphus does, since he never gives up despite his repeated failures. His actions ultimately have no meaning, and they never will have, but he never entirely loses hope.

The essay opens with a bold declaration: 'There is but one truly serious philosophical problem and that is suicide. Judging whether life is or is not worth living amounts to answering the fundamental question of philosophy.'[44] This is because Camus, in the tradition of existentialist thought, does not believe that life has any intrinsic value, so one needs to find or create some reason for going on with what is an absurd situation in which to discover oneself. Sisyphus comes to represent the dilemma that absurdity poses for humankind, and the daunting prospects it opens up for us. Repeatedly performing his allotted task but never succeeding in his objective, Sisyphus has to overcome the very natural urge to give up entirely, perhaps to take refuge in suicide. Going on under such adverse circumstances requires facing up to the sheer pointlessness of existence, but Sisyphus summons up the courage (or bloody-mindedness?) and becomes a symbol for all of humanity in managing to do so. Camus even claims that Sisyphus can be considered to embrace the task willingly enough, because it means he has taken responsibility for his actions and the direction of his life: 'His fate belongs to him . . . The struggle itself towards the heights is enough to fill a man's heart. One must imagine Sisyphus happy.'[45] It is a quintessentially pessimistic decision that has been made.

Sartre took over the notion of existential anxiety from Martin Heidegger, whose philosophy had a profound effect on him, and on French poststructuralism in its turn. Heidegger speaks of 'the "*thrownness*" of this entity [that is 'Dasein', or 'Being'] into its "there"', so that it is 'delivered over to its Being'.[46] 'Dasein' is therefore literally 'thrown *into existence*', but, crucially, this is '*not* of its own accord', hence the anxiety we feel at our situation.[47] Authentic existence is for Heidegger a case of being '*ready for anxiety*', the anxiety that understandably will come with having to entertain the possibility of one's own death.[48]

Heidegger is yet another post-Nietzschean thinker who calls into question the tradition of Western rationalism, although in his case the challenge has a tendency to take on an air of mysticism with this conception of the people as a racial entity (the *Volk*). This aspect of his philosophy was to draw him into the orbit of Nazism: just how much is a matter of some concern for his anti-fascist, poststructuralist and postmodernist followers. It demonstrates again just how varied the response to Nietzsche's pessimism could be: as we have noted, Adorno and Horkheimer's critique of rationalism led them to a rejection of Nazism. Heidegger's later work carries his critique of rationalism to the point of rejecting most of what Western philosophy stands for, which problematizes notions of truth and knowledge even further: 'It is time to break the habit of overestimating philosophy and of thereby asking too much of it. What is needed in the present world crisis is less philosophy, but more attentiveness in thinking.'[49] Poststructuralists like Jacques Derrida would be in full agreement with this attitude (as would the pragmatist philosopher Richard Rorty), which opens the door to a radical scepticism.

Poststructuralism and postmodernism are deeply controversial areas in contemporary philosophy, and opponents have even been known to complain that they are inimical to the whole spirit of philosophical enquiry, obfuscating rather than clarifying issues. The term 'Continental philosophy' has been coined to make sure we recognize that it is entirely separate from the supposedly more rational and logical Anglo-American, analytical tradition of philosophy: 'real' philosophy, as its proponents would have it. Adorno, not surprisingly, has proved to be a big influence on the 'Continentals'. As movements, poststructuralism and postmodernism are committed to challenging authority across the board, arguing that in every case it is going to be based on unsubstantiated assumptions. Both therefore seek to undermine our assumptions about argument and belief in particularly fundamental ways, pursuing a sceptical agenda about as far as might seem possible – well past the point of reason, in the view of their more vociferous opponents.

Few recent thinkers are capable of polarizing opinion quite as much as Jacques Derrida, the founder of deconstruction.

Derrida claims that we can never really trust language and that there is a continual and unavoidable slippage of meaning in its usage. Meanings, therefore, are not identical to themselves: a classic sceptical observation. This slippage occurs regardless of whether we are dealing with the written or the spoken word. Words just cannot be pinned down to an unambiguous meaning. They keep shifting and changing endlessly, even in the act of speaking or reading, deconstructing themselves as they go because they are marked by what Derrida refers to as *différance*:[50] that is, they always 'differ' from what we think they mean, and at the same time 'defer' the possibility of unambiguous meaning ever coming about. He makes extensive use of puns and wordplay to demonstrate language's inherent indeterminacy of meaning – the fact that 'writing . . . does not know where it is going'.[51] It is a practice which is felt to be philosophically highly questionable by his analytical opponents, however, who are just as bemused by his fondness for constructing an argument by way of parallel texts (see, for example, his somewhat notorious book *Glas*).[52]

Language, in Derrida's view, continually undermines itself, and in the process even the possibility of there ever being any 'agreed standard' for what could constitute 'truth' (a concept that sceptics, as we have seen, traditionally call into doubt). If it 'does not know where it is going', then it cannot specify how to judge its own validity. Deconstruction insists that we have to face up to the implications of this state of affairs, the main one being that received authority, in any field, lacks any stable foundations, so its credibility evaporates. For Derrida, this opens the way to ever more creative interpretation of texts and narratives (including those used by authority, such as ideologies), in what for him is 'a world of signs without fault, without truth, and without origin'.[53] To his detractors, however, it looks more like a state of anarchy in which communication breaks down altogether: what I have described elsewhere as a particularly radical form of scepticism, or 'super-scepticism'.[54] Philosophical debate would be impossible under those circumstances.

Jean-François Lyotard defines 'the postmodern condition' as the stage when we cease to be convinced by what universal theories – or, as he refers to them, 'grand narratives' – tell us about our world and how we ought to behave in it. According to Lyotard, we are now tending to adopt an attitude of 'incredulity' towards these instead, and he very much approves of this trend, arguing that resisting the power exercised by grand narratives should henceforth be the point of all politics.[55] Science, he feels, offers the basis for such resistance, with Lyotard arguing that research keeps undermining existing theories. This is particularly so, for example, in the weird and wonderful world of recent physics, which has yielded such strange phenomena as black holes, dark matter and dark energy. Science is, therefore, constantly 'producing not the known, but the unknown' nowadays.[56] (It is a conclusion one could also reach after reading the work of the astronomer John Barrow, who points out that there has to be a limit even to scientific knowledge; that our theories will always come to 'predict that there are things which they cannot predict, observations which cannot be made'.[57] Barrow goes so far as to argue that science could not exist unless this was so.) Most scientists, however, reject such a sweeping claim about their field, regarding it as a gross misinterpretation, and even outright distortion, of their practice – and of what their theories actually say.

But Lyotard does have more of a point when it comes to belief systems, such as political ideologies in general, which have come under a lot of attack in recent times, and often do elicit a very sceptical response to their assumed authority. Whether this applies globally is a moot point, but authority is far more likely to generate a response of 'incredulity' in the West than has been the case in most previous generations. The disconnect between the political class and the general public is now an accepted fact of contemporary life that politicians are prone to agonize over (without ever finding a satisfactory solution, revealingly enough). Lyotard is no longer prepared to accept that existing belief systems can bring about an end to injustice, or help us to change the world for the better. His own Marxist sympathies from his early career as an activist in the 1950s and '60s, for example, did not survive into later life, when disillusion set in with a vengeance, provoking him into some vicious attacks on the theory in works such as *Libidinal Economy*: 'We have no plan to be true, to give the truth of Marx.'[58] His solution is to look for pragmatic answers to any problem that may arise and to stop relying on received wisdom, such as Marxism or religion, as the unquestioned source of authority on what to do. We will seek those kind of sources in vain.

Nor is Lyotard optimistic that all disputes can in principle be overcome, and a compromise reached, just as long as the parties involved approach these in a spirit of reason. His line of argument in *The Differend* is that disputes – as in politics, say – all too often cannot be resolved, because they spring from the clash of incompatible worldviews, or 'differends', as he calls them.[59] The best that can happen in such instances is that the opposing sides respect each other's positions and agree to differ; the worst, that one side denies the other's validity and suppresses its claims by brute force. History provides us with copious examples of the latter happening, such as in Western colonialism.

Taking this line would mean that we have no precedents to fall back on, no basis for making value judgements, and this has proved to be one of the most contentious aspects of poststructuralist-postmodernist thought; arguably the one that has riled its critics above all. This has been a recurrent objection to scepticism throughout its history, and one can appreciate why so many would regard this as an alienating condition in which to discover oneself. It might seem to lead to fatalism – why bother doing anything at all if we have no overall system of values on which to ground our judgements? – even if this is not the conclusion that poststructuralists and postmodernists want us to draw from their claims. On the contrary, they regard these as liberating, arguing that their effect would be to free individuals from the control of others largely motivated by self-interest – dogmatists of one kind or another. As far as either movement is concerned, nothing has been determined beforehand. Everything is to play for.

Lyotard does, however, find reasons for pessimism when contemplating the issue of the Earth's lifespan, arguing in his book *The Inhuman* that it could lead to a turn towards developing computerised technology at the expense of human beings, in the hope that something would survive the event of the sun's 'heat death' even if humanity could not. It is a prospect that he considers 'inhuman', and he calls for a programme of resistance to be mounted against it in order to prevent the marginalization of humanity (the spread of computerization into all areas of human existence, and our increasing reliance on it, is already a source of worry among many commentators).[60] Fanciful though this all is, the notion being that the corporate interests controlling techno-science might regard this as a new 'grand narrative' to promote, it does show that philosophical pessimism sees no limit to its range of application. The worst is always there on the horizon, wherever it looks, and it wants us to be prepared for that. There is certainly no reason to assume that the corporate sector can always be trusted to put humanity's interests first when making a commercial decision.

Michel Foucault is another Continental philosopher to argue the case for resistance to grand narratives, regarding most of the institutional systems we have developed in the modern age as instruments of the ruling class's desire to keep the population under its strict control. Prisons, hospitals and asylums are notable cases in point: 'There is, in these institutions, an attempt to demonstrate that order may be adequate to virtue', and of course that is virtue as interpreted by those imposing the order.[61] Power in general becomes the target of Foucault's cultural critique, and he is a spirited defender of the underdog and all those who do not succumb to the ruling elite's pressure to conform – such as the insistence on heterosexuality as the only 'natural' form of sexual expression. In the latter respect, Foucault turns into one of the leading advocates of gay rights, helping to inspire what has come to be known as 'queer theory' in works such as his three-volume *The History of Sexuality*, which traces the development of sexual norms and behaviour from classical times up to the present day. In his wide-ranging analysis, Foucault's concern is to locate the roots of sexual repression, claiming that we have not yet really overcome this, even in our supposedly liberal and tolerant modern world:

> Why do we say, with so much passion and so much resentment against our most recent past, against our present, and against ourselves, that we are repressed? By what spiral did we come to affirm that sex is negated? What led us to show, ostentatiously, that sex is something we hide, to say it is something we silence?[62]

As a member of the gay community, Foucault was more likely to be aware of the prejudices that sex could still arouse in our culture, and the mechanisms of power underlying these, than most. He is not at all optimistic that everyone will now automatically receive equal treatment regardless of their sexual orientation: this still has to be fought and campaigned for vigorously.

There is an underlying pessimism to Foucault's analysis of how power operates in our culture, and why it is so successful in suppressing opposition. Most people will go along with what the ruling powers dictate, and will incorporate their ideas into their own worldviews and lifestyles. We know, for example, that homosexuality is still frowned upon by many in our own society (the Christian church has considerable problems with it), and is illegal in many parts of the world, where it can lead to imprisonment and harsh sentencing. We tend to accept the institutions the ruling powers set up, and adhere to the norms that they create. Where other thinkers might identify consensus, and consider this a sign of a well-ordered society, Foucault sees something more like a conspiracy to keep the populace in line through enforced conformity. Few will risk their own safety by voicing dissenting opinions or behaving differently from the masses; it is almost as if we have an intrinsic desire to conform and can be quite easily led. It was this tendency that frustrated Adorno above all, because without at least tacit collusion, neither mass political systems nor mass culture would work.

Foucault wants us to resist conformity, and to work to promote a diversity of lifestyles within our culture, without discriminating against minority groups. But he fully recognizes how uphill a struggle this can be, how habituated we have become to the institutionalization of our culture on behalf of a dominant group. He does not believe it to be a lost cause, however, because ideas can change: power is not immutable, and no system is impregnable. Rather like Adorno, he challenges the ideas that came out of the Enlightenment movement, and their supposed benefit to Western culture ('man' as a uniquely rational being, and so forth), but he can see its influence eventually withering away. He can even speculate on 'the death of man':

> As the archaeology of our thought easily shows, man is
> an invention of recent date. And one perhaps nearing
> its end. If those arrangements of our thought were to
> disappear as they appeared, if some event of which we
> can at the moment do no more than sense the

possibility – without knowing either what its form will be or what it promises – were to cause them to crumble, as the ground of Classical thought did, at the end of the eighteenth century, then one can certainly wager that man would be erased, like a face drawn in sand at the edge of the sea.[63]

It is an arresting image, but unlike, say, Marxist theorists, Foucault cannot say what might bring about this radical cultural change, and there is a certain amount of pessimism to be detected in his assessment. Marxists may remain optimistic about how to engineer a new kind of social order, but Foucault cannot accept that it could be so straightforward. Like a true pessimist, he does not assume the 'right' outcome, only its possibility, hence that strategic use of 'perhaps'. His perspective on history is that it reveals how difficult it can be to step out of the mainstream, but he will go on recommending that we do just that nevertheless.

Richard Rorty's pragmatism is often identified as being close in spirit to Continental philosophy (Rorty is clearly sympathetic to this movement), and it shows again that the key principles of scepticism need not lead to an attitude of fatalism. Like sceptics in general, Rorty accepts that we can never reach absolute certainty with regard to our knowledge, but thinks this is more of a reflection on the discipline of philosophy than on our minds. In his view, this means that the terms of the debate have to be altered significantly. The question we should be asking those who claim to be in possession of certainty is not how they know this, but 'Why do you talk that way?'[64] In other words, what are they trying to gain through their claims? (as far as poststructuralists are concerned, the real answer should be 'to gain power over others'). There will always turn out to be a set of beliefs lying behind any such pretension to certainty, but for Rorty some beliefs are more interesting and useful than others, and it is those he is trying to tease out and champion (interestingly enough, he thinks they are more likely to be found in literature than philosophy, so the next chapter ought to yield some for us to mull over). It should not matter to us whether we can ever be certain about their 'truth' or not – Rorty echoing scepticism's dismissive attitude towards this concept – only what effect the beliefs in question will have on what we think or do. He is very critical of his own discipline, adopting a position that has been described as post-philosophical.

What this means for the pessimist is that sometimes our predictions about those effects will prove correct, and the worst will happen (probably most times, in fact), but sometimes they will not and the worst will not occur. So 'work, worry, toil and trouble' notwithstanding, you just have to get on with it; pessimists can live with that, it is only what they expect out of the existence anyway. There is no magic formula to guarantee how the future will work out, and that is a point that postmodern philosophers are constantly making. No theory or programme can ever manipulate the future to its liking, as Marxists were only too confident theirs could; what Lyotard dubbed the 'event', the totally unexpected and unpredicted occurrence that may not at all be to theorists' or politicians' liking, can always intervene (a revolution, stock market crash or natural disaster, say). Lyotard describes this in dramatic fashion as 'the impact, on the system, of floods of energy such that the system does not manage to bind and channel this energy; the event would be the traumatic encounter of energy with the regulating system'.[65] Optimists would most likely be taken by surprise; pessimists would regard it as just another episode of the worst – unfortunate, yes, but to recall one of Kurt Vonnegut's favourite asides, 'so it goes'.[66]

Identity becomes a very fluid phenomenon for post-structuralist and postmodernist philosophers, who see it as continually in a process of change, 'becoming' instead of 'being'. Rather than individual identity being a stable entity, we adopt a series of roles as we move through life, constantly becoming something other than we were. This can be disorienting to others, but fits in with the view taken of language by such thinkers, for whom it cannot be tied down to specific meanings. Just as truth can never be established beyond doubt, neither can meaning nor personal identity. Although post-structuralists and postmodernists argue that this is liberating, it does demonstrate yet again the limits of our knowledge.

At the opposite end of the ideological spectrum we find Roger Scruton's take on pessimism, in his book *The Uses of Pessimism and the Danger of False Hope*. Scruton sets out to expose the various fallacies that underpin irrationalism and unreason, with his particular target being those 'unscrupulous optimists who put their belief in abstract scheme[s] for human improvement'.[67] Schemes of this kind, as in communism or fascism, are anathema to someone of Scruton's conservative political outlook – as is even the social democratic form of socialism. As I pointed out in chapter One, I do not share Scruton's political conservatism (the left is full of optimists, in his opinion), and I suspect that many of the types of pessimism considered above would strike him as examples of unreason in action. My own pessimism stems from a very different interpretation of the left's history that still sees the need to keep its ideas in play in an era of neo-liberal domination. Indeed, it is the continued existence of conservatism on the Scruton model that is one of the sources of my pessimism. I find his focus far too narrow, therefore, but I do agree with him that we need to be on our guard against unscrupulous optimists of all descriptions. Personally, I think we should be more worried about the optimists on the neo-liberal right and their market fundamentalist zealotry, which surely does qualify as an 'abstract scheme for human improvement', and a particularly insidious one at that.

* ✳ *

I would argue that scepticism shows the way to the more positive form of pessimism being recommended in this book, encouraging an attitude of incredulity towards the more fanciful claims of optimists that humanity's dark side can become a thing of the past. This stops short of Schopenhauer's more extreme version, which I do feel overstates the problem. I would rather we act as if the worst was always a very live possibility (if not as definite as Schopenhauer contends), and that things will continue to happen which our theories 'cannot predict', whether these turn out to be the result of human actions, of the kind we have become so distressingly familiar with over the ages, or the vagaries of the natural world. Climate change represents a deeply worrying combination of the two, and it will take more than mere optimism about human ingenuity to make it go away – even if optimists seem to have an almost limitless faith in the power of science and technology to save the day. A scepticism-informed pessimism would argue that we cannot simply turn a blind eye to such evidence, and I really do not think that we should.

FIVE

A World Without Meaning:
Pessimism in Literary Fiction

Pessimistic visions abound in the world's literary fiction, and although there will be a bias here towards the tradition that I imagine readers are likely to be most familiar with, that of the West (and particularly the English-speaking branch), every literary tradition would readily yield its own examples. Writers of fiction have to be highly observant of human behaviour, from the public to the private, and that can make them very sensitive to the problems that beset us as individuals, as well as to the psychological and character failings that can create, or exacerbate, so many of those problems in the first place. Not surprisingly, this often leads to a rather jaundiced attitude to humanity and what it has to contend with in life, lending a gloomy and pessimistic air to their work.

It would be impossible to cite every last indication of pessimism in the history of literary fiction here, so I shall be exploring a selection of some of the most prominent works. These will be taken from various periods – from classical Greece up to the present day, Greek tragedy through to American crime fiction – with the objective of demonstrating just how ingrained pessimism is in our cultural history, and the extent to which it has informed the creative imagination down through the ages. In each case, a pessimistic worldview plays a vital role in the narrative, and that view continues to have a powerful resonance with readers of our own time, who struggle to come to terms with the kind of issues raised in the opening paragraph of chapter One. Each era has its own version of these issues, and we can learn from how others have tried to make sense of them by capturing them within a fictional framework to show the implications they had for individuals' lives. Those fictional frameworks help to clarify just what the problems are, and form case studies for us in that respect, no less than works of philosophy do. Fiction can, and should, be a source of knowledge that we can apply to the world around us, and I shall proceed on that basis.

* * *

The belief in classical Greece was that the gods could control affairs in the human world. Human beings were thus no more than mere playthings in their schemes, and the clear message was that we were not, and never could be, in full control of our own destinies. Individuals would ultimately find the odds stacked against them, no matter how much success might have come their way beforehand. In Sophocles' *Oedipus Rex* we witness the tragic events that can result when our fate is out of our own hands. The story is well known, and gave its name to Freud's concept of the 'Oedipus complex', which keeps its themes alive in the modern world. It has also been a source of fascination and inspiration for generations of artists and composers since classical times (Igor Stravinsky's oratorio-style setting of the text, adapted by Jean Cocteau, is a notable example from the twentieth century).

Oedipus is abandoned by his parents just after his birth because of a doom-laden prophecy: 'Apollo's oracle had nothing but ill to foretell of him: he was destined one day to kill his father, and become his own mother's husband.'[1] Left to die on a mountainside, Oedipus is, however, rescued from his fate by a shepherd, and eventually becomes prince of Corinth. Unwittingly, he does slay his father, Laius, when they clash as travellers on the open road. Then, when he is attracted to Laius' widow, Jocasta, Oedipus woos and marries her, unaware that she is his mother. All this is as foretold by the oracle. Oedipus and his family are reduced to the status of pawns manipulated by the gods, who are determined to avenge an earlier crime committed by Laius when he violated the hospitality of his host by raping one of his sons. Crucially, this is also a violation of a law laid down by the gods, and punishment must inexorably follow. Laius has to be held to account, and the gods must exact an appropriate revenge. When the gods decide it will, then the worst does indeed occur, and human beings cannot affect the outcome, no matter what they may try to do. It is that sense of the absolute injunction to revenge a wrong, and of the inevitability of the fate of those who have committed it, that was to leave its stamp on the development of revenge tragedy as a genre.

Revenge goes on to play a significant role in drama and literary fiction in England from the sixteenth century onwards, when its framework enabled authors to articulate some of the most pressing social and political problems of the period in a thought-provoking manner. Revenge tragedy became a particularly popular form in Elizabethan and Jacobean drama, attracting some of the most important playwrights of the period, such as Christopher Marlowe, William Shakespeare and John Webster. In such works, as J. R. Mulryne points out in his introduction to one of the earliest English revenge tragedies, Thomas Kyd's *The Spanish Tragedy*, 'justice and revenge interact', and they do so in a complicated and frequently confusing manner that poses serious questions about the morality of individuals taking the law into their own hands.[2] That interaction can also be noticed at work, and just as problematically, in contemporary crime fiction.

In Marlowe's *The Jew of Malta*, the revenge theme centres on the merchant Barabas who, along with his Jewish compatriots, is ordered to hand over half his estate to the governor of Malta in order to pay a tribute levied by the Turks on the island. Refusal will mean being forced to become a Christian.

When he protests against this demand, Barabas's entire estate is seized (although he manages to retrieve some of it by subterfuge), leading him to swear that he will 'be reveng'd upon the Governor'.[3] Some can find it a depressing play. In his introduction to an edition of the complete plays of Marlowe, J. B. Steane speaks of 'the almost unredeemed meanness, weakness or wickedness of the people and their actions' in a world marked by 'villainy, hypocrisy, [and] pettiness'; although he does concede that the protagonist is nevertheless a lively character whose adventures succeed in holding the audience's attention.[4]

Barabas proves to be a master of dissembling, as his many asides to the audience readily reveal. He justifies his conduct on the grounds that, 'It is no sin to deceive a Christian.'[5] His devious plotting leads to the death of the governor's son, as well as his daughter Abigail's love, Don Mathias, thus turning her against her father. When she becomes a nun to spite him, Barabas swears revenge on her too. The frenzied scheming soon involves the death of a friar, who is strangled by Barabas and his servant, then double-dealing on Barabas's part between the Turks and the Maltese. His treachery uncovered, Barabas is lured to his death by the governor of Malta, and is plunged into a boiling cauldron. The play's farcical quality (it is rather like a demented pantomime by the end) can jar given the gory events taking place. As it so often does in revenge tragedy, life seems cheap, and that does not suggest a particularly optimistic view of human nature. The willingness of everyone to exploit others for their own ends is what registers more strongly than anything else in this play; this is human nature at its worst, and the audience cannot fail to pick up the underlying pessimism about human existence that it communicates.

Several of Shakespeare's plays can be placed in the category of revenge tragedy, running from such grisly works as *Titus Andronicus* to arguably his most famous, *Hamlet*. Titus exacts terrible revenge on the empress's sons Chiron and Demetrius for having raped and maimed his daughter Lavinia: he has them slain and then baked in a pie which is served up to their mother at a feast organized by Titus. This is one of the more ghastly acts of vengeance in the genre's history. Hamlet is told by his father's ghost that he was poisoned by his uncle Claudius so that he could become king of Denmark and wed Hamlet's mother. It is another heinous crime that cries out for revenge, and the necessity that Hamlet should be the agent of this throws him into a state of considerable metaphysical confusion, revealed through a series of anguished soliloquies ('To be, or not to be', and so on). Ultimately, he does carry this act out, but at the cost of his own death.

If it is not as sensational as Marlowe's venture into revenge tragedy, this is nevertheless a drama where meanness of spirit and self-interest play a worryingly large role in many of the characters' lives, as well as one with considerable emotional and metaphysical depth. Hamlet's melancholy demeanour is a response to this display of the less savoury side of human nature, and the sense of insecurity it brings into individuals' lives. He becomes an interestingly representative figure of the period in this respect, since something of a spirit of melancholy began to creep into English culture in the face of the many uncertainties of the late Elizabethan era. The monarch's childless state meant there was no clear successor to the throne, leaving the country vulnerable to political intrigue, which may well have led to its religious settlement coming under threat from Catholicism. This was a fear that carried on into the Jacobean regime that eventually came to power, and melancholy became a noticeable phenomenon in intellectual circles in reaction to such problems.

Hamlet is only one of several malcontents to be found in Shakespeare's oeuvre, which also include the figures of Iago in *Othello* and Edmund in *King Lear*, both of whom feel they have been denied their just reward in life. They turn into schemers who plot tirelessly behind the scenes to advance their own cause, creating mayhem and misfortune in the lives of others around them. Any sympathy that the audience might initially feel for their plight is soon dissipated by the calamitous effects of their actions on those who have trusted them. The validity of revenge is clearly being called into question in these plays. As the genre prescribes, death has to be their punishment.

Arguably the most powerful representation of the malcontent in this dramatic tradition is the character of Bosola in John Webster's *The Duchess of Malfi*. Bosola has come to have a very pessimistic view of human nature after suffering repeated disappointment at the hands of the eminent figures who employ him, such as the Cardinal, the Duchess of Malfi's elder brother. Having seen his own initial good nature repeatedly taken advantage of by his social superiors, he has now decided to put self-interest first and seek his own advancement, even if this has to come at the expense of the misery of others, none of whom he really trusts any more. 'What creature ever fed worse, than hoping Tantalus; nor ever died any man more fearfully, than he that hop'd for a pardon?', as he rhetorically enquires of an acquaintance.[6] He is now described as the 'court-gall', positively consumed by 'foul melancholy', although there is a certain amount of sympathy expressed at the beginning for his unfair treatment.[7]

Bosola, however, sinks further and further into evil as the action unfolds, arranging the Duchess of Malfi's death at the apparent request of her brother Ferdinand, who then refuses to reward him and banishes him from Malfi instead. Outraged by yet another show of ingratitude, Bosola takes his revenge on the brothers in a subsequent struggle, with all three of them – in the best tradition of the genre – ending up dead. Yet again, it is the cheapness of human life that leaves the most lasting impression, and the audience is left to speculate on just how widespread belief in this might be. The play leaves you feeling more than a bit uncomfortable.

I suggested in chapter One that pessimism is quite consistent with black humour, and a particularly striking example of that can be found in *The Revenger's Tragedy* by Cyril Tourneur (although the play's authorship has been disputed). The play forms a counterpart to the revenge tragedies discussed above in its madly comic tone, tracing the antics of the revenger Vindice and his considerable talent for dissembling. 'For to be honest is not to be i'th' world', as he justifies it, and there appears to be no-one around in the play to contradict that judgement.[8] Gruesome deaths occur at regular intervals throughout the action, and for all the comic treatment (which comes across as a sort of 'Carry On Revenging'), the underlying ethos is nihilistic. This is a world that is seemingly incurably corrupt, where truth and justice have no place, no-one can be trusted, and where human life counts for very little. The humour is about as black as it could be, and it radiates the sense of pessimism that underpins revenge tragedy. There will be no glossing over of the faults of humanity, the dark side of human nature, in this tradition.

* * *

The profound impact that melancholy had on the literary sensibility of the late Elizabethan and Jacobean periods was to be repeated in the eighteenth century. It can be seen to particularly good effect in the work of Laurence Sterne, best known for his novel *The Life and Opinions of Tristram Shandy, Gentleman*, which disguises a pessimistic worldview behind comedy and a sentimental attitude towards life. The main point being made in *Tristram Shandy* is a serious one: that we have little, if any, control over our individual lives, which appear to be ruled by chance, rendering Tristram 'the continual sport of what the world calls Fortune'.[9] Any scheme set in motion by either Tristram or his father never works out as intended, and sometimes with hilarious consequences. Tristram is christened with precisely the name his father is most determined to avoid, thanks to a series of small mistakes which lead to his actual choice, Trismegistus, becoming garbled as it is communicated down the line to the officiating clergyman.

Tristram's life is accident-ridden right from the moment of his conception, owing to his mother raising a mundane household matter at the critical point of his father's ejaculation, leading, as his father sees it, to his 'animal spirits' being scattered in a random manner, thus denying his son the ability to develop a coherent identity.[10] From then on, the accidents accumulate, and chance rules Tristram's life at every turn. 'Whatever can go wrong will go wrong' well describes Tristram's subsequent career. 'We live in a world beset on all sides with mysteries and riddles', as the hero is forced ruefully to admit.[11]

Sentiment becomes Tristram's way of dealing with a world that seemingly conspires against him, manifesting itself in a sense of pity and concern for the misfortunes of humanity in general. All of us are assumed to be prey to the workings of chance, to the apparently inevitable deflection of our intentions towards some unlooked-for effect. The worst does keep occurring in this universe, and all we can do is to acknowledge this with the best grace we are able to summon up, and get on with life within those problematical parameters. Pain and suffering, for example, are simply part of human existence and must be experienced, and then lived through, by us all. That is our destiny. Sterne's characters are capable of breaking out in tears when confronted by such situations, even stories about them, as happens to both Tristram and his uncle Toby. In fact, Sterne started something of a cult with sentimentalism, and 'Shandeism', as it came to be known, soon became fashionable with certain impressionable young men among his readership.

Sterne qualifies as a pessimist, therefore, though one able also to appreciate the comic side of the human condition; black humour appears in the book in the most literal fashion, with a black page symbolizing the death of one of its characters, Yorick. Perhaps there really is nothing more to say about death than this, especially if, unlike Sterne, you happen not to be religious. Sterne has a knack of treading a fine line between comedy and tragedy. At one point Tristram is accidentally circumcised (or so it seems, anyway) by a falling sash window, just after his nurse has placed him upon its ledge; the window's system of pulleys have been weakened by the removal of parts commandeered by his uncle Toby for a mad engineering project he is engaged upon. Uncle Toby is quite possibly castrated (the text remains coy on this) by a series of knock-on effects from a bullet that ricochets from a castle wall when he is part of a besieging force there in a war. The worst can strike with terrifying suddenness, but all you can do is look back on such events wryly.

* * *

Russian culture can provide a host of reasons for being pessimistic about the human lot. It is a country with a very unhappy, as well as bloody and violent, history, with the last century alone featuring a communist revolution, purges and famines, that could only encourage an attitude of pessimism on the part of the ordinary citizen. Even now, in the post-communist era, its population has to cope with large-scale political corruption, authoritarian rule and a poorly functioning economy. Optimism hardly thrives in such circumstances. Nor did it in the nineteenth century under an oppressive czarist regime and an autocratic ruling class, and it is in this milieu that Fyodor Dostoevsky's work is set. *Crime and Punishment* has to be one of the gloomiest novels in Western literature, and its vision of human nature is almost unrelievedly pessimistic, much of the time to the point of nihilism.

Crime and Punishment's Raskolnikov is a character disillusioned with an existence of grinding poverty as a student in St Petersburg, dependent on handouts from his mother and sister. He lives in a slum area of the city inhabited by a motley collection of drunks, prostitutes and down-and-outs, none of whom seem to have any prospect of an improvement in their condition. It is a world and way of life to which he feels no loyalty, and he is only too representative of the discontent that was building up in the country at the time, especially among the young, generating several rebellions and terrorist outrages against the rulers before the 1917 revolution which finally toppled the old order.

Raskolnikov's own prospects offer him no grounds for hope. His mother cannot go on borrowing against her small pension in order to send him money indefinitely, and he cannot accept the scheme that she and his sister Dunya have concocted, whereby she will marry a middle-aged suitor she does not love purely to improve the family's financial situation and pave the way for Raskolnikov to be taken on by the suitor in his law practice on completion of his studies. Raskolnikov's outrage at this humiliating turn of events leads him to conceive of a scheme to murder a pawnbroker in her apartment in order to rob her and so alleviate his situation, making it unnecessary for his sister to make her sacrifice on his behalf. Despite his desperate financial plight, and even though the pawnbroker is not a particularly nice personality, it is still a callous and senseless act that reveals a very distorted set of moral values on the part of the protagonist: 'a Hamlet without a clearly identifiable cause', in the words of one of the author's translators.[12] Raskolnikov's sense of morality goes from bad to worse in the deed's aftermath and, on being discovered by the pawnbroker's sister while still in their apartment, he feels compelled to murder her too to prevent her from going to the police to report him.

The vision of existence presented by Dostoevsky is unrelievedly gloomy and pessimistic, with St Petersburg presented as being full of shifty characters who make up the time's version of the precariat (soon to be mobilized by the communist movement), living in a squalid environment of dirty, crowded alleyways and desperately cramped living conditions. Dostoevsky is a notoriously elusive author to pin down, as commentators are prone to point out, and it is difficult to determine exactly what moral he wants us to draw from such a narrative (for all Raskolnikov's apparent redemption by its end), or where his own sympathies lie. But its overall oppressive atmosphere is unmistakably pessimistic, picturing a society where much of the population feels it has nothing to look forward to, no relief from a depressing round of 'work, worry, toil and trouble'. It is manifestly not a context likely to inspire finer feelings to grow, and Raskolnikov's reaction to being trapped there becomes understandable. There is a powerfully claustrophobic feeling to the novel.

Whether the hero's spiritual awakening could ever excuse such an action as murder is another matter, as is whether this is anything like as important to readers nowadays as it clearly was to Dostoevsky or his contemporary Russian audience. Sacrificing others in a bid to improve your own pessimistic outlook does not look morally defensible. It is the character's psychological turmoil that continues to fascinate a later readership, rather than the message of Christian optimism that concludes the narrative.

The Idiot is another gloomy narrative that casts human nature in a very poor light. Humanity is presented as essentially mean and grasping, and characters like the saintly and idealistic Prince Myshkin, 'an out-and-out holy fool', as another character slightingly refers to him on first making his acquaintance, simply do not fit in.[13] The novel is a chronicle of the progressive disillusionment of what the author referred to in a letter as 'the positively good man'.[14] Russia is depicted as a corrupt, immoral society where money is worshipped and idealism is out of place. Even Myshkin is tarnished by all of this by the novel's end, his faith in humanity all but destroyed by his repeated encounters with characters who systematically lie, cheat and even kill to gain an advantage over others. Given the almost unrelieved sense of doom and gloom that prevails throughout Dostoevsky's work, it is unsurprising that he was described by a contemporary reviewer as 'a cruel talent'.[15]

* * *

At the time Thomas Hardy was writing, Schopenhauer's ideas were much in vogue in intellectual circles, and he was certainly familiar with the work of that thinker: one commentator pictures him 'working his way industriously through Hegel and Schopenhauer in the Reading Room' of the British Museum.[16] Hardy himself was to deny that he was a pessimist, and he could write comic novels, but elements of Schopenhauer's work do appear to come through in both his novels and poetry. The notion of the 'Immanent Will' that plays such a key role in Hardy's aesthetic vision, for example, suggests Schopenhaurean influence. 'Work, worry, toil and trouble' do seem to be the lot of many of his main protagonists as well, with Tess Durbeyfield and Jude Fawley being prominent examples. Tess is exploited by almost everyone she meets: by her family (for her labour when young, then her beauty as a desirable young woman who might succeed in improving their fortunes by marriage); by Alec D'Urberville (who rapes her); and by the farmer who employs her after she is rejected by her husband, Angel, when he discovers she is not a virgin (as a consequence of her rape). Eventually, having murdered Alec in revenge, she is pursued by the forces of the law and then hanged after her capture and subsequent trial.

With biology, social background and social convention all stacked against her (Schopenhauer's deadly combination of nature and nurture), life seems to be almost totally unforgiving towards Tess, offering nothing more than fleeting moments of happiness along the way. There is the courtship sequence at Talbothays Dairy, in spring and summer, for example, where 'Tess had never in her recent life been so happy as she was now',[17] and Tess's reconciliation with Angel in the immediate aftermath of Alec's murder. The implication is that this is all we can really hope for out of life: brief respites from the dispiriting daily grind. Something unpleasant always lies in wait just around the corner.

Jude proves to be yet another victim of social background and stultifying convention. His ambition to be a scholar at university level is frustrated at every turn, as there simply is no route into higher education at the time for someone of his lowly social status. (On a personal level I can readily sympathize with such a character, having become a mature student after working as a tradesman in the printing industry. Jude has no such opportunity open to him.) He is forced to accustom himself instead to a life of constant disillusionment, and has to recognize that his initial sense of optimism about the future was horribly misplaced. Suicide blights Jude's life when his young son does away with himself and the other children, with the pitiful justification offered in his final note to his father: 'Done because we are too menny.'[18] Again, 'work, worry, toil and trouble' form the insistent backdrop to Jude's existence, with no real escape from this desperate sequence apparently being available, only fleeting moments again. Like humanity in general, he can only stumble on from misfortune to misfortune as circumstances conspire against him, dying a defeated man. It is a tragedy that unfolds slowly and painfully, but just has to be suffered through: that is the human lot.

Hardy's poem 'The Convergence of the Twain (Lines on the Loss of the Titanic)' also pictures human beings as caught up in the actions of uncontrollable outside forces, and punished for their presumption that they could ever contrive to overcome these and be the authors of their own fate. The development of the iceberg and the boat's construction are seen to parallel each other in a deeply mysterious, yet seemingly inevitable manner that leads them towards each other on the open sea:

> Till the Spinner of the Years
> Said 'Now!' And each one hears,
> And consummation comes, and jars two hemispheres.[19]

Doom seems to lurk permanently on the horizon of Hardy's world, and humanity just has to accommodate itself to that discomforting knowledge. If things can conspire against us, then they surely will at some stage; that is the way of the Immanent Will. Schopenhauer could only agree, although Hardy does allow for some lighter moments occurring on the route there, which is some comfort at least.

* * *

The slaughter and carnage of the First World War generated an air of pessimism among many of the poets serving in the armed forces – a sense of the utter futility of it all that eventually overrode the optimism that politicians had so successfully whipped up at the war's beginning: 'it will all be over by Christmas', and so on. Wilfred Owen's work from that period is particularly affecting in this regard. The images can be uncompromisingly stark, as in 'Cramped in that Funnelled Hole':

> Cramped in that funnelled hole, they watched the dawn
> Open a jagged rim around; a yawn
> Of death's jaws, which had all but swallowed them
> Stuck in the middle of his throat of phlegm.
>
> They were in one of the many mouths of Hell
> Not seen of seers in visions, only felt
> As teeth of traps; when bones and the dead are smelt
> Under the mud where long ago they fell
> Mixed with the sour sharp odour of the shell.[20]

The exuberant sense of optimism that had led so many to join up to fight for the national cause in 1914 is definitely missing here, with the poet's disenchantment only too clearly evident. This is war carried well beyond glory, to the point of being terrifying and inhuman; not a message that the nation's leaders would want to hear at all. It was a message, however, that was increasingly to come out of the conflict from figures like Owen.

Siegfried Sassoon was another poet to turn against the war, and he became particularly notorious for his 'Soldier's Declaration' of 1917, in which he stated his opposition in the plainest possible terms:

> I am making this statement as an act of wilful defiance of military authority, because I believe that the War is being deliberately prolonged by those who have the power to end it. I am a soldier, convinced that I am acting on behalf of soldiers. I believe that this War, on which I entered as a war of defence and liberation, has now become a war of aggression and conquest . . . I make this protest against the deception which is being practised on them.[21]

The authorities did their best to hush this up, and had Sassoon hospitalized for suffering a nervous breakdown, but the statement was merely a logical extension of the anti-war sentiments that were increasingly coming through in his poetry. The gap between political rhetoric and the reality of life in the trenches could not be denied indefinitely: optimism can only go so far. Reading the war poets can still be a disturbing experience today, especially now that we are far more sensitive to the phenomenon of post-traumatic stress that combat can cause.

* ✳ *

Few works of literary fiction offer a more pessimistic vision of human nature and our psychological make-up than William Golding's *Lord of the Flies*, which sees our dark side as deeply embedded within us right from childhood; in effect, as innate. All it requires is the right set of circumstances and it will inevitably manifest itself, as it does here when a shipwreck projects a group of adolescent boys back to the equivalent of the Hobbesian 'state of nature', where they are forced to fend for themselves. Bullying and dominant behaviour do not take long to emerge in this context, and the community soon divides into exploiters and exploited. The stronger characters turn into a pack of hunters, displaying a taste for killing that eventually makes them turn on the weaker members of the group.

Upon rescue, the British naval officer who discovers them remarks incredulously that, "'I should have thought that a pack of British boys – you're all British aren't you? – would have been able to put up a better show than that – I mean –'", eliciting only the lame reply that "'It was like that at first . . . before things –'".[22] But Hobbes would not have been surprised by the rapid decline into atavistic behaviour once social controls had been loosened, and Golding would appear to be just as pessimistic about human nature. War tends to have much the same effect, releasing an otherwise suppressed capacity for brutality that only requires the right set of 'things' to occur to come into play.

* * *

Existentialism has had a notable impact on literary fiction, promoting an essentially pessimistic vision of the human condition. In Albert Camus' *The Plague*, a powerful metaphor for the Nazi Occupation in France during the Second World War, life goes on even in the face of daily setbacks and the constant threat of sickness and death – much as it had in occupied France. Neither can we ever rest easy, because we are never really free from that threat: 'the plague bacillus never dies or disappears for good . . . it can lie dormant for years and years'.[23] We may well 'learn in a time of pestilence . . . that there are more things to admire in men than to despise' (although it is doubtful that philosophical pessimists like Adorno would have agreed), but we have to recognize that 'pestilence' is nevertheless the inescapable backdrop against which we must conduct our lives.[24]

The protagonist of Camus' *The Outsider*, Meursault, is a figure who seems unable to overcome the absurdity of existence and create meaning within his life. His attitude is summed up in his reaction to an offer from his employer in Algiers of a transfer to Paris, where there would be the opportunity to have a more exciting time than in the sleepy provinces: 'I told him I was quite prepared to go; but really I didn't care much one way or the other'.[25] By Sartre's standards Meursault is guilty of bad faith, drifting through the world without committing himself to anything: as he remarks at one point, he is someone who has 'rather lost the habit of noting my feelings'.[26] After an altercation on the beach with two Arabs who wound a friend of his, Meursault returns to the scene, and when the remaining Arab draws a knife on him he shoots him in quite a callous fashion. In prison he feels no sense of remorse, his main concern being 'how to kill time'.[27]

The trial seems to hinge more on Meursault's character than the actual act of murder he has committed, and it is his apparent callousness and lack of normal human feelings (he is not even able to make himself pretend to have these in order to generate sympathy in the jury) that condemn him. He is sentenced to be executed. It is only on the point of death that his existence comes to mean anything to him, Meursault remarking that he 'felt ready to start life over again', and that he can now say he is 'happy'.[28]

Samuel Beckett's work also has a distinctly existentialist edge to it, and his oeuvre can be considered a sustained exploration into the pointlessness of human life. His pessimistic credentials are neatly summed up in his aphorism: 'Do not despair, one of the thieves was saved; do not presume, one of the thieves was hanged.'[29] In other words, one must never give up, but must always be aware that a bad ending is only too likely. Nevertheless Beckett believes we should carry on even in the face of the repeated failure of our efforts: 'Ever tried. Ever failed. No matter. Fail again. Fail better.'[30] The burden of the pessimistic temperament could hardly be more neatly captured.

Pessimism is the permanent backdrop to the characters' lives in Beckett's world, which appears to have absolutely no meaning to it and where nothing much ever happens no matter how long they wait. His characters are stranded in limbo wondering what to do with themselves, and what the point is of doing anything at all. Thus in *Waiting for Godot* Vladimir and Estragon keep telling each other that they should go, but in every case the stage direction that follows says '*They do not move*', and that is how the play ends; nothing has been achieved, nothing has been resolved.[31] The comic tone of much of the action cannot disguise the bleakness of the human condition, which is summed up by Pozzo when he observes: 'They give birth astride of a grave, the light gleams an instant, then it's night once more.'[32] That sequence may well be what is being demonstrated in Beckett's most enigmatic play, *Breath*, which consists merely of the sound of a 'Faint brief cry' followed by a raising and then dimming of the theatre lights on a stage 'littered with miscellaneous rubbish.'[33] And that is it; the whole play lasts less than a minute.

Yet, crucially, Beckett's characters continue waiting for something to break the monotony, and to find some meaning in their existence. At the end of *Krapp's Last Tape* the character semi-defiantly declares: 'Perhaps my best years are gone. When there was a chance of happiness. But I wouldn't want them back. Not with the fire in me now. No, I wouldn't want them back.'[34] Perhaps there is something of the heroism that Camus finds in the life of Sisyphus in a sentiment like this, as there might be also in the insistence of Winnie at the end of *Happy Days* that 'Oh this *is* a happy day, this will have been another happy day! After all. So far', despite there being nothing to justify that conclusion but another day of monotony, chattering away to Willie and listening to his monosyllabic replies.[35] The mere fact of Willie talking to her at all is enough to convince Winnie that it will be a happy day; better than nothing at all happening. As usual with Beckett's characters, they are marking time until the worst of all finally arrives.

* ✳ *

Crime raises very awkward questions about human nature. Although it varies in incidence and type, it is a consistent presence in every society around the globe, as it has been throughout recorded history. At best, it can only be said that all societies manage to achieve is to keep it in check to a greater or lesser extent; it never goes away entirely, and this is both a source of fascination and worry to authors of crime fiction and their readers. Crime fiction in general has a pessimistic cast, therefore, in that it pictures a world where crime and human venality keep recurring and would appear to be impossible to eradicate. Murder is very often the focal point of such fiction, and even if the culprit is eventually tracked down and punished, it does present a very unflattering image of the human race: individuals are all too ready to give into greed or take revenge into their own hands. Nevertheless, the fact that the murderer is brought to justice in some fashion (either by death at the point of discovery, or capture followed by trial and prison) suggests that order can be brought back into the world and that crime does not pay. There is a moralistic dimension to such fiction, therefore, even if it is only implicit, to go along with its undisputed entertainment value.

In recent years, however, crime fiction has begun to take on a more disturbing tone. The concern is to show that our institutional systems – justice, law and order, politics, personal conduct – are collapsing around us, leaving traditional moral codes in tatters. This is very much the case in American crime fiction, where a series of authors have been producing a stream of works which suggest that achieving justice through legal means has become all but impossible in contemporary America. When and if it does come, justice is at best rough-and-ready, giving little indication of a world in which law and order can prevail on any long-term basis; social decline is simply too far advanced, public and private morals just too corrupted. Optimism is clearly in very short supply.

Again, only a selection of authors can be dealt with here, but in the novels of James Ellroy, James Lee Burke and George Pelecanos – all highly respected figures in the field – there is a powerful sense of a culture in freefall, in which justice can only be effected through revenge and vigilante activity, normal channels having ceased to cope in any efficient manner. In the works of these authors, pessimism about human nature would appear to be a given, and it is a pessimism that can even shade into a kind of nihilism about their nation's future prospects. With so many greedy and self-interested human beings around, operating in a culture where such traits are openly encouraged to drive the economy on, that future can only look bleak.

America has always been a violent society, as Ellroy makes abundantly plain in the 'LA Quartet' of 1987–92: *The Black Dahlia*, *The Big Nowhere*, *LA Confidential* and *White Jazz*. The Quartet is centred on the Los Angeles Police Department (LAPD), which is presented as a den of corruption, alcoholism and drug-taking. Justice is largely dealt out by vigilante action on the part of the LAPD's detectives, the author's own phrase for this method being 'absolute justice'. This is what comes into play when even a corrupt, amoral detective feels that a certain line has been crossed: a criminal has to be made to pay for some particularly horrific act, or acts, of violence, even if it involves taking the law into the detective's own hands. Thus in *LA Confidential*, Bud White, a detective suffused with violent impulses, takes revenge on wife-beaters, having witnessed the death of his own mother at the hands of his violent father.

The moral standards of the LAPD are little better than those of the local criminal class, with precious little suggestion of social responsibility on view among its officers, other than their somewhat dubious belief in 'absolute justice'. Absolute justice is a concept whose implementation merely serves to reinforce the desperate cycle of violence that grips American big-city life. It is justice conceived of on an 'eye for an eye' basis. The implication is that this is the only way to cope with crime in a society whose institutions are in a state of disarray, and whose functionaries are frequently corrupt and motivated by self-interest and greed rather than public service. But since absolute justice depends on an individual decision, and an emotional one at that, mistakes can be made. Innocent members of the public are sometimes killed, and even if it is a criminal who is the mistaken target, that fails to resolve the issue as it leaves the guilty party at large and thus still a danger to society.

Almost everyone in Ellroy's work has something to hide. Ed Exley, for example, is a decorated war hero when he first joins the LAPD and an apparently principled individual, yet we are later to discover that he is a fake on this score, having pretended to have performed actions he did not. He is the son of former high-ranking LAPD officer Preston Exley, whose advice to Ed on the advent of his police career involves the recommendations to fabricate evidence against suspects if he is sure they are guilty, or to be prepared to beat confessions out of them, even to kill them, rather than arrest them. His acknowledgement of 'the brutality of crimes that require absolute justice' hardly suggests he is to be considered morally principled either.[36] The detective Jack Vincennes once accidentally killed some bystanders while high on drugs on duty, and he also has an arrangement with the local gutter press for them to photograph him making high-profile celebrity arrests that are set up in advance. The attendant publicity gives him an entry into the burgeoning world of television as a consultant on a serial about the LAPD, *Badge of Honour*. Vincennes's heroism is therefore no less faked than Ed Exley's. It turns out that the star of *Badge of Honour* is a paedophile. No-one at all can with confidence be taken at face value in Ellroy's world – there is generally something shameful in their personal history – and his fiction certainly qualifies as pessimistic about humanity in general.

Ellroy's vision brings to mind Hobbes's state of nature yet again, with egocentric individuals completely obsessed with their own interests to the exclusion of all others. It is a ruthless, unforgiving environment, and for Ellroy it pretty much sums up the state of America right through to our own day. Not the least of the many ironies in his work is that the 1950s are generally looked back on as a golden age in modern American life that compares very unfavourably to the present in terms of moral standards. Ellroy's line, on the other hand, is that violence and immorality are so deeply and destructively embedded in American life that the 1950s were no different from our own time. In reality there was no supposed golden age, no matter what the surface appearance may imply. Therein speaks a true pessimist.

The Black Dahlia takes us back to LA in the 1940s. The title comes from the name of a real-life unsolved murder case of the late 1940s that drew sensationalized press coverage at the time. Detective Dwight Bleichert becomes obsessed with the case, pursuing it long after the force has given up for lack of clear evidence as to the identity of the killer. Obsessiveness in the cause of absolute justice is a trademark trait of Ellroy's detectives, but it will always find itself up against the official tendency to sweep anything unpleasant and harmful to its image under the carpet, and to prefer appearance to reality.

The Big Nowhere and LA *Confidential* move the action to LA in the early 1950s. In the former, the city authorities are whipping up anti-communist campaigns to counteract the ideology's supposed infiltration into American life through areas like the film industry. The narrative marks the rise to prominence of Lieutenant Dudley Smith, a key figure from then on in the Quartet. Smith turns out to be a very un-pleasant and untrustworthy individual whose cunning proves too much for most of his colleagues, whom he is only too willing to undermine, to the point that their reputations in the force are destroyed. The main victim of his machinations in *The Big Nowhere* is the detective Danny Upshaw, a closeted homosexual in denial about his feelings, who lives in constant fear of being outed by his rabidly anti-gay police colleagues. Upshaw is a highly intelligent and efficient officer, but this counts for nothing as his boorish colleagues' suspicions about his true sexuality gradually grow stronger over the course of the narrative – yet another indictment of the force's militantly conformist and insular culture. In LA *Confidential*, a station Christmas party erupts into a savage mass beating by the officers of prisoners in the station's cell block. It is only when this is reported by the local press that any action is taken, but in most cases this goes no further than enforced early retire-ment or brief suspension from duty. Violence and corruption are everywhere you look, as with the bribe-taking protagonist of *White Jazz*, Detective Dave Klein.

James Lee Burke's 'Dave Robicheaux' series, based around the career of an ex-alcoholic police detective, first in the New Orleans Police Department (NOPD) and then in the smaller nearby town of New Iberia, Louisiana, becomes progressively darker and more pessimistic in tone as the series develops. The most recent novels in this long-running series have a distinct tendency towards apocalyptic endings, Robicheaux usually accompanied in these ventures by his ex-partner in the NOPD, Clete Purcel. Purcel is an ongoing alcoholic who left the NOPD with his reputation in shreds, later becoming a private detective. In neither guise does he show much respect for the rule of law, remaining very much a rogue individual, liable to be led by his emotions into rash actions at almost any moment. Unable to allow himself to take refuge from the world in alcohol any longer, Robicheaux turns instead to his surroundings, the lyrically described bayous of southern Louisiana, where he fishes and engages in reflection on the dark side of human nature that he keeps encountering in his work. This strong identification with his local environment means that he can only react with dismay as he observes the adverse impact on it made by the creeping incursions of big business, notably the oil industry.

Both Robicheaux and Purcel have deep-rooted violent impulses that need little prompting to come boiling up to the surface, causing mayhem. Savage beatings are dealt out to career criminals at the slightest pretext, and these proliferate over the course of the series as Robicheaux's sympathy with his culture is systematically eroded by the criminal behaviour and corruption he sees occurring, and apparently being tolerated, all around him. Guns and violence, deployed in vigilante fashion, become the default position in the search for justice; little else gives the impression of working effectively any more. For Robicheaux, America has lost its way and become a mere shadow of its former self, and his complaints about this state of affairs become more numerous and voluble as the series develops – as does his nostalgia for what he perceives to be the kinder world of his youth. A similar nostalgia pervades Burke's other crime series based on the career of the police detective Billy Bob Holland in Montana. Holland, too, becomes sadder, and angrier, about how the once-pristine state environment is being changed by the activities of the corporate sector and the intrusion of the criminal class. There is a feeling of a paradise being spoiled in both of these series.

The Tin Roof Blowdown, set during the Hurricane Katrina episode, radiates pessimism about human nature, including that expressed through government and its elected officials (a favourite target of Burke's), felt by many to have failed New Orleans very badly in its hour of need. In Burke's uncompromising assessment, 'one of the most beautiful cities in the Western Hemisphere was killed three times, and not just by the forces of nature.'[37] In the stricken city after Katrina hits, Robicheaux finds a scene where looting is rife, casting human nature in a very bad light. He also finds evil on the loose in figures like Ronald Bledsoe and his associates, who leave a trail of crimes and murders behind them. Again, we are left with a sense of how thin the veneer of civilization can be – by no means the perception of an optimist.

George Pelecanos's Nick Stefanos trilogy (*A Firing Offense*, *Nick's Trip* and *Down by the River Where the Dead Men Go*) features yet another burned-out individual, this time a compulsively drug-taking, semi-alcoholic private detective. Stefanos's life is a mess of binges where he staggers from bar to bar, followed by brief spells of sobering up – binges that get steadily more epic as the trilogy develops. By the last book of the trilogy, *Down by the River Where the Dead Men Go*, he is having frequent blackouts during the binges and looks to be on an irreversible downward spiral: a broken man seemingly hell-bent on self-destruction. He is barely able to hold down a job anymore, having sunk to the level of being a bartender in a down-at-heel Washington bar, the 'Spot'.

Stefanos is sympathetic towards those at the bottom end of the social scale, as in the population of Washington's African American ghettoes, and how they are being ruthlessly exploited by the city's corrupt politicians and businessmen. Recent surveys have indicated that the city is one of the most unequal in the country in economic terms, with an affluent minority – connected in some way or other to the capital's political culture (politicians, high-ranking government officials, lawyers, corporate lobbyists and so on) – and beneath that a majority (until recently anyway, it has been declining) African American population with some of the lowest average earnings in the USA. There are two Washingtons, therefore: one a glamorous tourist destination and seat of international political power, the other squalid and drug- and crime-ridden, looking more like the developing world than part of the richest nation on Earth. Stefanos gives every impression of a character who is unable to deal with the injustice of this any more, and takes refuge in drugs and alcohol as readily available means of escape.

Nick is surrounded by acquaintances who appear at least as unable to cope with daily life without the prop of drugs and alcohol, Johnny McGinnes being a prime example. We first meet the pair in *A Firing Offense* when they are both salesmen in Nutty Nathan's, an electrical goods store that stands as a symbol of American-style capitalism at its least attractive: aggressively hard-selling, concerned only with parting the customer from his or her money, and pushing its sales staff to the limit in order to outdo their competitors. McGinnes's solution to surviving through the day in this deeply unpleasant environment is to engage in regular interludes of drug hits and alcohol consumption. Nick's lifestyle is little better, and *A Firing Offense* ends with Nick out on a binge, behaviour that will become only too characteristic of him.

Nick's Trip finds him ensconced at the Spot and only taking on casual PI assignments, having decided that he cannot face becoming a full-time PI in a professionally run agency, which would require him to straighten out his increasingly chaotic lifestyle. A request from a childhood friend to help him find his lost wife turns into an alcohol-fuelled road trip that goes badly wrong, ending in the discovery that his friend has lied to him and lured him into the trip on false pretences.

Although his friend pays for this deception with a prison sentence (if a short one), it is yet another unpleasant lesson to Nick in just how little he can trust human nature. Most of the people he encounters are concerned with furthering their own interests at the expense of others, and will do whatever it takes to bring this about.

Nick's work as a PI plunges him into the seedier side of Washington life, turning him into an ever more desperate character unable to cope with what he sees happening around him, and the binges become noticeably more dramatic. The one that kicks off the action in *Down by the River* finishes with Nick passing out on a river bank, having staggered there from his car, oblivious as to where he is. His only memory of this episode when he wakes up in the morning is of hearing some mysterious noises in the night that he later discovers were caused by the murder of a young African American man by drowning. Nick's conscience at having been nearby when this happened, but unable to do anything about it because of his drunken condition, prompts him to look further into the case – which is soon dropped by the local police, in line with a generally casual attitude towards the murder of young African American men.

The investigation carries him into the murkier side of the city's underworld, revealing a network of drug rings and porn film-making that lures in the local African American population, who are otherwise trapped in dreadful housing conditions and with minimal employment opportunities. Nick can make precious little difference to the overall situation, and his frustration leads him to take his vengeance out on a white Washington businessman, Richard Samuels, who has moved into the drug trade that has the African American ghettoes in its merciless grip. Samuels's defence of his actions, 'I'm a businessman, after all . . . Simply put, I saw the demand in the market', enrages Nick to the point where he executes Samuels while in a rage about his callous attitude.[38] When Samuels tries to gain Nick's sympathy by parading his religious belief, it is to no avail: "'Oh God,' he said as I drew the Browning from behind my back. "There isn't one," I said, and shoved the barrel into his open mouth. "Remember?"'[39] It is absolute justice in action yet again, and as in Ellroy's novels it seems the only possible way left for the protagonist to register the depth of his anger at the apparent collapse of moral values in his culture.

* ✳ *

In the mid-nineteenth century several novelists began to produce what came to be known as 'Condition of England' novels, all of them addressing the serious problems that had arisen in recent English history due to famine and the rampant spread of industrialization throughout the country. Notable contributors to this sub-genre were Charles Dickens and Elizabeth Gaskell. Dickens's *Hard Times* and Gaskell's *Mary Barton* in particular paint sombre pictures of the damaging effect of industrialization on the populace and the environment. Both are set in Lancashire, one of the heartlands of the English Industrial Revolution. Alienation from one's labour is much in evidence among the working class of the time. Interestingly enough, these two novels unfold much in the manner of crime fiction, with a murder lying at the heart of the plot.

Despite a generally critical tone, the 'Condition of England' novels nevertheless held out the hope that society could change for the better; they are by no means recommending Marxist-style solutions. So they are only pessimistic up to a point, still retaining some faith that the better side of human nature will win through and prepare the way to a happier society. The crime novelists we have just looked at, however, could be considered to be producing 'Condition of America' narratives, constituting a sub-genre far more pessimistic about the prospects for their culture than their nineteenth-century forebears, one that almost seems past rehabilitation. Nor are they alone in helping to establish a new sub-genre, with some of the most distinguished authors in the country taking a similarly pessimistic line about American culture: Cormac McCarthy and Philip Roth are cases in point. The novel has become one of the primary vehicles of social criticism in American culture, and it is not a particularly pretty picture that emerges.

McCarthy's work can be very bleak in its assessment of the American lifestyle, and less than complimentary about human nature's role in creating it, culminating in *The Road*, with its apocalyptic setting so reminiscent of Hobbes's state of nature. Earlier, in *The Border Trilogy* and *No Country for Old Men*, McCarthy explored the effects of the violence and greed that have come to play such a large part in modern American life, eating away at the nation's value system.

The Border Trilogy is set in the American-Mexican border-lands over a period of generations, with characters crossing back and forth between two very different cultures, encountering cruelty and exploitation of the weak by the strong, the poor by the rich, on both sides. It is a harsh and fairly desolate landscape where life is hard. You have to be constantly on your guard against others, never sure how much you can trust them: every encounter could spell danger. A Mexican Yaqui, Quijada, explains to one of the American protagonists, Billy Parham, how a popular old song 'tells the tale of that solitary man who is all men. It believes that where two men meet one of two things can occur and nothing else. In the one case a lie is born and in the other death.'[40] Mexico is pictured as a more backward society than America, a country where violence is never far away; not that it is absent across the border in Texas either. Violent death proves to be an unremarkable occurrence in either society. It is not an environment, in other words, to encourage the development of finer feelings.

No Country for Old Men presents a very unattractive vision of modern American society, particularly its obsession with money and the lengths people can be willing to go to for this. Evil, represented by the figure of Chigurh, is a very real factor in society, and violence simply an everyday occurrence that the population has come to treat with resignation. Sheriff Bell represents an older, more honourable style of life, but he is weighed down by the cumulative experience of the violent acts he has encountered throughout his career. He is a man reduced to sadness by what American culture appears to be turning into; someone out of time. Visiting a prisoner on Death Row for a murder of which Bell had helped convict him, Bell cannot understand his lack of remorse for the crime, reflecting that:

> He was not hard to talk to. Called me Sheriff. But I didnt know what to say to him. What do you say to a man that by his own admission has no soul? Why would you say anything? I've thought about it a good deal. But he wasnt nothing compared to what was comin down the pike.[41]

What turns out to be 'comin down the pike' is characters like Chigurh, who stalks the landscape like an angel of death, cold-bloodedly killing anyone who is an impediment to his objective of pursuing and retrieving the money stolen from an aborted drug deal in the desert that left several dead.

The money has been taken by a local resident, Llewelyn Moss, who came across the crime scene while out hunting. He is unable to resist the temptation it offers, and after being spotted at the scene and shot at, decides to make a run for it with the unexpected windfall of over $2 million. Greed is a powerful motivator that can undermine moral codes very quickly. What he doesn't know is that the satchel containing the money has a transponder in it, and that Chigurh is able to follow it wherever it is carried, using a receiver. A cat-and-mouse chase through the borderlands and over into Mexico ensues, with predictably violent results and a trail of dead bodies. It is yet more evidence to Sheriff Bell of a society whose moral values are collapsing, and it leaves him feeling defeated and beaten, no longer able to understand what is happening to his culture.

The Road traces the journey of a father and son, in search of a safe haven after some nameless disaster has hit their country, rendering it all but uninhabitable and leaving only small pockets of humanity scattered around the ruined landscape. There is no evidence of a central government left and human society has broken down. As in Hobbes's state of nature, life has turned into a desperate daily battle for survival, with the strong exerting their power over the weak. Almost none of the older human, civilizing values remain in circulation, with the father's sense of responsibility towards his son being a very notable exception. Generally speaking, whoever else they meet on the road proves to be untrustworthy, out to save themselves even if it has to be at the expense of others' welfare, willing even to resort to cannibalism and slavery to make this possible.

Neither does the ending dispel the general air of pessimism infusing the narrative. The father dies, his duty towards his son done in reaching their destination on the coast, where he can join a like-minded commune of people. Yet even though the son's prospects are better than they were, there has to be a lingering doubt about his future – and that of the human race as a whole. Whether society can ever reconstruct itself, and evolve from the state of nature it has been projected back into by events unknown, has to remain a very open question.

Philip Roth's fiction has a misanthropic, often misogynistic edge to it that has become more pronounced as his career has developed. *The Plot Against America*, for example, a counter-factual narrative about Charles Lindbergh defeating Franklin Roosevelt by a landslide in the 1940 Presidential election, detects a nasty undertone of fascism in American life. Lindbergh's campaign makes it clear that he is against intervening in the Second World War on the Allied side, and that he considers the American Jewish community's apparent support for such an action unpatriotic and counter to the country's best interests. On election, he establishes friendly relations with Hitler, reaching "'an understanding" guaranteeing peaceful relations between Germany and the United States.'[42] Life becomes progressively more awkward for American Jews from that point onwards, with the Nazi leadership trying to interfere in American domestic politics.

The turn of events Roth describes has a definite air of plausibility, and it says some unflattering things about the right in America, which is a particularly powerful political force in our own day. It suggests that he thinks it would not take much to bring anti-Semitism to the surface in American life, and that the country may not be as tolerant as it publicly prides itself on being: a melting-pot of nationalities and beliefs. It is a fairly pessimistic verdict on American culture, and Roth's late novels paint an unflattering portrait of human relations there. He often picks apart gender relations, as in *Everyman*, whose protagonist is successful at his job, but anything but when it comes to his private life, having gone through three failed marriages and alienated his two sons in the process. A combination of poor health and ageing is making him uncomfortably aware of his own mortality (a recurrent theme in late Roth): 'They were all embarrassed by what they'd become. Wasn't he? By the physical changes. By the diminishment of virility. By the errors that had contorted him and the blows – both those self-inflicted and those from without – that deformed him.'[43] As the title indicates, this is what awaits all of us who live long enough, and there are echoes of Schopenhauer in such reflections on the impending 'worst of all'.

David Kepesh, the elderly critic and academic in *The Dying Animal*, sleeps with a succession of his female students, justifying his conduct on the grounds that 'I'm very vulnerable to female beauty, as you know. Everybody's defenseless against something, and that's it for me. I see it and it blinds me to everything else. They come to my first class, and I know almost immediately which is the girl for me.'[44] It is the kind of excuse that men are only too prone to put forward for their conduct, and although he is often criticized for the portrayal of women in his novels, Roth can be very critical of the male sex as well. There are no unflawed protagonists in his work, and he can sound at least as misanthropic as misogynistic in tone. This is a writer only too attuned to human weakness, particularly as it reveals itself in the American character. *The Human Stain* takes further aim at gender relations (with Coleman Silk yet another aging lecher to add to the list), as well as political correctness and race relations, and the catalogue could go on. Roth has a pretty jaundiced view of humanity and its ways, and the 'condition of America' in his fiction is not at all praiseworthy.

* ✳ *

The pessimism being expressed in the works above seems only too justified by the situations being described, and the plight of those who are caught up in them. There is an overall impression given of life as a trial, but in the absence of any viable solution to that quandary – the existentialist dilemma: if life has no meaning then neither can suicide – there is no alternative but to continue on with existence as long as one is allowed to do so. 'Work, worry, toil and trouble' simply cannot be avoided. It is true that the authors above have chosen to document the lows largely at the expense of the highs, and, yes, others of their peers do the exact opposite and can find justification for their decision too. Yet even if life is perhaps not quite as bad as Schopenhauer found it (I hope not, despite my commitment to pessimism), it nevertheless has a significant proportion of lows that can prove wearing to even the most resilient of characters. The popularity and staying power of the fiction that displays that process in operation – and, as pointed out before, this is but a small sample of it – suggests that there is a very sizeable audience of readers keen to consider how interpretations of it relate to their own experience. We may not agree with every author's vision, but we can certainly learn from their engagement with pessimism and consider how we may have reacted instead to such distressing circumstances.

SIX

Visions of Despair:
Pessimism in the Arts

The visual arts have been no less sensitive to the many seemingly intractable problems facing humanity over the years, and artists too have often gravitated towards the pessimistic end of the spectrum of human behaviour. War, violence, human failings and powers outside our control have affected artists as deeply as they have authors, with a host of works throughout the visual arts bearing testament to this. Music, too, can express a pessimistic worldview, from classical through to popular, the symphonic to the blues tradition, and that topic will be where my survey of pessimism's aesthetic dimension concludes.

* ✳ *

From Francisco Goya's *The Disasters of War* to Pablo Picasso's *Guernica,* the horrors of war have shocked artists into responding with equally shocking images. While war once was glorified to a large extent, being considered a stage upon which acts of heroism were performed, the modern era has been more inclined to dwell on the suffering and destruction it has caused, as both Goya and Picasso depicted so power-fully. War photographers are in many ways carrying on Goya's work in our own day, providing images of the devastation that armed conflict always leaves in its wake. These ensure that we are left in no doubt as to what 'the disasters of war' can involve at a human level.

Goya's paintings and engravings of the Spanish War of Independence against the French (1808–14) portray a world of carnage and human suffering that is extremely distressing. There is no sense of glory in these works; instead we are presented with the harrowing plight of the victims of pointless violence, as in *One Can't Look* from the *Disasters* series, where the scene is of a massacre of Spanish civilians by French soldiers. In Gwyn A. Williams's description, 'they die without heroism or dignity and yet there is something inexpressible about the manner of their dying which makes it an obscenity'.[1] *The Third of May 1808* captures yet another massacre by the French, and such scenes proliferate throughout *Disasters*. The series is full of ghastly images of the dead and dying, the obscenity of it all jumping out at the viewer; images by which Goya 'fixed forever the evil deeds of a pitiless oppression'.[2]

The political situation in the Spain of the period was confusing, with reactionary and modernizing forces arrayed against each other. French revolutionary ideas found a fair amount of support in the country, especially among those of a liberal tendency, turning the 'War of Independence' into a civil war as well as one against the alien French invaders. Goya does not shy away from showing the atrocities committed by Spaniards against their own countrymen, and gives the impression of someone whom experience has rendered 'irredeemably pessimistic' about human nature.[3] Once hostilities begin and our destructive impulses are brought into action, then violence begets yet more violence, and the situation can soon spiral out of control; as war poets were only too aware.

'Visions of Despair' is an apt way of describing the work of Edvard Munch. Both *Despair* and *The Scream*, painted in 1892 and 1893 respectively, radiate an intense sense of pessimism about the human condition, as Munch's own reflections on the source of inspiration for the paintings clearly indicates:

I was walking along a path with two friends – the sun was setting – I felt a breath of melancholy – Suddenly the sky turned blood-red – I stopped and leant against the railing deadly tired – looking out across flaming clouds that hung like blood and sword over the deep blue fjord and town – My friends walked on – I stood there trembling with anxiety and I felt a great, infinite scream through nature.[4]

An optimist would no doubt have seen a spectacular sunset, probably worth waxing lyrical over, as Romantic poets were wont to do, but Munch turns the scene into an Expressionist nightmare. It is the vision of someone of whom it could be said: 'He suffered, and depicted the condition of modern man, in a time which was not yet conscious of its own predicament. Furthermore, he proclaimed this predicament to be the content and meaning of his art.'[5] In *Despair* the moment is caught just as Munch had described it, with a figure looking out over the fjord and two other figures walking away from him on the left of the canvas. None of their faces can be made out clearly, and it is the menacing blood-red clouds that attract the attention. In *The Scream* the foregrounded figure may even be the source of the scream (and at the very least appears to be joining in), which reverberates like a howl of anguish about the modern world. The lurid colour scheme and swirling lines intensify the impact, and there is a feeling of dissolution and breakdown about the composition, which, as one curator of Munch has put it, 'has become an icon for the anxiety and loneliness of modern people'.[6] Munch himself was to suffer a nervous breakdown in later life.

Similar feelings of anguish and despair can be found in the plays of Munch's compatriot Henrik Ibsen, who depicts a sensation of being trapped in a society where the social conventions are severely restricting the individual's horizons and stifling personal development. Appropriately enough, Munch was to design the stage sets for some productions of Ibsen. For the Swedish playwright August Strindberg, *The Scream* represented nature's 'rage', which is 'about to speak through storm and thunder to those foolish, puny beings who imagine themselves to be gods without resembling gods'.[7]

Munch was later to call another of his works *Despair*, this time as part of a series of lithographs entitled *Alpha and Omega* (1908-9), for which the artist provided an accompanying narrative with echoes of the Adam and Eve story. Again there is a background of wild, swirling lines around the central figure, Alpha, whose despair at being deserted by Omega is mirrored in the landscape as described by the artist: 'Heaven and earth were the colour of blood. He heard screams in the air and covered his ears. Earth, heaven and ocean trembled and a terrible fear possessed him.'[8] On Omega's return, he kills her, a pointer to the level of distrust that can develop between the sexes, perhaps because of their essential incompatibility (some critics detect a misogynistic streak in Munch, and his relations with women do seem to have been somewhat problematical). Death is to crop up as a theme in many of Munch's works, and there is a dark and brooding atmosphere to much of his output, carrying very pessimistic overtones: 'Nordic noir' indeed.

Before Picasso's *Guernica* burst onto the scene, the First World War was to produce its own crop of artists who felt driven to capture the horrors witnessed there, in a conflict that resulted in an unprecedented amount of slaughter. One of the most prominent of these was the German Otto Dix, who went from being a fervent patriot who joined up at the outbreak of war in 1914, to an artist out to shock his audience with gruesome images of war's consequences. In a series of prints titled *Der Krieg*, Dix pictured such things as a human skull crawling with worms, and the uniformed skeleton of an unburied soldier propped up against the wall of a trench. There is nothing like the spirit of jihad on display here; more of a waste of human life in what proved to be a doomed cause.

Dix's painting *The Trench*, depicting a tangle of blown-apart bodies that prefigures *Guernica*'s more abstract composition, was later to be included by the Nazis in their infamous 'Degenerate Art' exhibition of 1937. This was hardly surprising, given the movement's ideological glorification of war as the means to establishing the supremacy of the 'master race'. A warlike disposition was taken to be a sign of commitment to the Nazi project. This meant that Dix's imagery was far too pessimistic in its view of human nature, and the cruelty it could inflict when its worst side was unleashed by war, to find favour in a Germany that by then was gearing up to fight in order to redress its defeat in the First World War. The painting itself has since disappeared, and is only known from surviving prints.

Other German artists to take a strongly anti-war stance in their work were Ernst Kirchner and John Heartfield. Then there was the Dada movement, which began in neutral Switzerland during the First World War, being motivated in the first instance by an extreme reaction against the war. It was a reaction uncompromising enough to reject all the traditions that had produced war, including the canons of what could actually count as art. Dadaists deliberately refused to make sense in their creative activities, deploying chance and randomness much of the time. One could also regard this as pessimism at its extreme; a wholesale rejection of cultural history and all that it stood for. European civilization itself is being held accountable, and treated with complete disdain.

Dix's post-war work in general, like that of many of his contemporaries such as George Grosz and Max Beckmann, has a deep vein of pessimism running through it and is highly critical of the mores of a contemporary German society which seemed determined to pretend that the war and its horrors had never really happened. Unfortunately such views, very much constructed in the shadow of the horrors of war, were soon to be overridden by yet another instance of the worst of human nature asserting itself in the rise of the Nazis with their warlike intentions. Given the continued incidence of bloody wars over the rest of the twentieth century and then on into our own, it is small wonder that pessimism keeps reasserting itself. War can give no cause for optimism, no matter what our political leaders may want to claim (think of Henry v's rousing speech on the eve of the battle of Agincourt: 'and gentlemen in England now a-bed / Shall think themselves accurs'd they were not here, / And hold their manhoods cheap whiles any speaks / That fought with us upon Saint Crispin's day' (Act iv, Scene iii)). We still await the 'war to end all wars', and nothing on the current scene, with its many intractable disputes over territory, sovereignty and ideology, gives much cause to believe that there is the necessary will to bring this about. Iraq, Afghanistan, Ukraine and the Middle East, to name just the most obvious cases at present, inspire little confidence in the ability of opposed belief systems to reconcile their differences. Intolerance continues to break through, regardless of past lessons as to where this can lead. We really do need to keep consulting paintings like the above to remind us.

Glorification of war and violence is a defining characteristic of fascism, and it can be found in the work of the Futurist movement in Italy, which yielded some very problematical art, considering the socio-political context in which it was produced. Futurism's founding manifesto of 1909, by the poet F. T. Marinetti, declared: 'We will glorify war – the world's only hygiene – militarism, patriotism, the destructive gesture of freedom-bringers, beautiful ideas worth dying for, and scorn for woman.'[9] Even the experience of the First World War did not dampen the Futurists' enthusiasm, and many became involved with the rise of fascism in Italy under Mussolini, allowing their own Futurist political party to be subsumed under the latter's leadership. There could not be a more startling counterpoint to the views of Goya, Dix and

Picasso than this when it comes to the effects of war and violence. Or to the Dada movement: whereas Dadaists sought to cut themselves off from the past because of the war it had brought, Futurists did so in order to establish war as the very basis of modern culture. Whether one could find anything of value in Futurist art if you did not share their values is a very open question. It can be difficult to detach the image from its inspiration.

Few paintings better sum up the social and political turmoil of the twentieth century than Picasso's powerful masterpiece *Guernica*. The fractured bodies scattered every which way on the large canvas reveal a society torn apart by internal hatred, enough to set its citizens against each other in quite merciless fashion in a civil war, which ended in the triumph of fascism under the repressive regime of General Franco. It would not be until after Franco's death in 1975 that Spain could throw off this yoke and re-enter the mainstream of European life as a properly democratic nation. *Guernica* is not very characteristic of Picasso's work, which is rarely this sombre in tone, nor as overtly political in theme and intention. True, some of the work of his earlier 'Blue Period' has a sad and melancholy air to it, such as paintings like *The Tragedy* and *La Vie*. The etching *The Frugal Meal*, from the same period, also communicates that kind of feeling in the figures of an impoverished couple. But Picasso is more often praised for the life-affirming quality of his phenomenally inventive oeuvre, with its frequent changes of style and artistic direction. That is not what we find in *Guernica*, which positively seethes with anger about the depths to which human nature is capable of sinking. It is an anger that can also be found in a work completed just before *Guernica*, the etching *The Dream and Lie of Franco*, which depicts Franco as a grotesque figure.

Guernica was a response to a bombing raid on the Basque town of that name, carried out by German planes supplied by the Nazis in support of Franco's fascist cause. Those responsible tried to shift the blame onto the opposing Republican forces, claiming they caused the damage (there are some striking parallels with what happened over the MH17 plane crash in Ukraine in 2014, with both sides insisting it was the fault of the other). The painting was Picasso's response, although its effectiveness as a political statement was a controversial issue from the start. The influential art critic Clement Greenberg, for example, one of the greatest champions of modernism, was not impressed at all. Another critic has argued that '*Guernica* is a *vague* painting. Nobody knows what is going on in it, and it is the merest literary double-talk to maintain that this is what gives it universal application.'[10] The sentiments that inspired Picasso to create it, however, are not in doubt; neither is the fact that it has retained its anti-war, anti-fascist connotations over the years. It is difficult to imagine the work being discussed without reference to its historical context; it seems inescapably tied to that. That is the way it has been presented to the public in most exhibitions, and it would seem perverse to treat it as a purely abstract work of art. As with Futurism, it is not at all easy to separate image and inspiration.

Joan Miró was another artist very much opposed to fascism, and he produced several anti-fascist posters during the Spanish Civil War, such as his striking *Aidez L'Espagne* (1937). He was only one of several artists to produce propaganda posters for the socialist Republican side, which also drew many writers to its cause – George Orwell being a notable English supporter. Orwell bewailed the atrocities of the war, and admitted they were committed by both sides (if more frequently by the fascists), but nevertheless felt the Republican cause was just, that 'it was a class war' and that he knew which side he was on.[11] Conceding that 'war is evil', he nevertheless insisted that it was 'often the lesser evil' – a far cry from fascist glorification (compare it, for instance, with the sentiments in the Futurist Manifesto).[12]

In a far more downbeat mode to the call to 'aidez l'Espagne', however, there is Miró's *Man and Woman in Front of a Pile of Excrement*, painted just before the Civil War broke out, one of a series of works produced by him around this time that have been given the name *peintures sauvages*. For Roland Penrose, these are emotionally intense paintings depicting a 'nightmarish reality'.[13] Collectively they are considered to express the artist's fears about the way events were shaping up in Spain, and a growing pessimism about the likely outcome to the political turmoil. It is a pessimism which proved, sadly enough, to be only too well-founded. Penrose finds the 'violence of Miró's feelings' about the deteriorating political situation in the run-up to the Second World War coming through in various other works of the late 1930s, such as *Woman's Head* and *Seated Woman I*.[14]

* * *

Ingmar Bergman's films unmistakably communicate an air of pessimism. This attitude is often considered to be a characteristic of the Scandinavian countries, as the stream of so-called 'Nordic noir' book and television series over the last few years would also suggest. In Bergman there is a sense that we now live in a godless universe, with nothing more to look forward to but death awaiting us at the end. This comes through powerfully in his most famous film *The Seventh Seal* (1957), in which a knight, Antonius Block, returning to Sweden from the crusades, challenges Death (a hooded figure in black) to a game of chess with his life as the stake. Trying to find solace in his Christian faith, the knight comes to feel that God is no longer listening to humanity's complaints: 'I call out to him in the dark but no one seems to be there.'[15] Death's somewhat malicious comment on this, 'Perhaps no one is there', can only sow further seeds of doubt about the point of existence in the knight's mind.[16] Yet the knight continues to engage in the chess game in the forlorn hope that he can still manage somehow to escape his fate, to win against Death: precisely what I take to be the reaction of a pessimist.

All of this takes place against a background of plague, and the civil disorder following on from its ravages, lending the narrative a particularly sombre feel. When a parade of flagellants passes through, it merely seems to sum up the powerlessness, yet residual hope, of the human race in the face of disaster. Rather in the mode of existentialism, humanity is trying desperately to make sense of existence in the absence of any transcendental meaning. Death has more reality than God, who may indeed not be there. The film ends with a dance of death on the horizon from victims of the plague: the ending that awaits all of us, whether we are struck down by the plague or not. Death always wins.

Bergman's films are often seen as sustained explorations in the dilemma of having to exist in a universe without God to give us a system of values against which we can regulate and judge our conduct. It is a dilemma that his characters struggle with but can never resolve satisfactorily, spending their lives in a state of varying degrees of psychological torment and unease. In *The Silence* (1963), for example, the main characters are stuck in an unnamed country where they cannot even speak the local language, thus emphasizing their lack of meaningful contact with others – and by extension, God. Yet again 'no one seems to be there', and in Bergman's world that removes the possibility of optimism about the human condition. As in Sartre's existentialism, we are very much alone and that can only be a cause for anxiety.

Nordic noir has also found a ready home on television, with series like the Danish *The Killing* attracting a worldwide audience (as well as spin-off versions in other countries like America). Henning Mankell's 'Inspector Wallander' books (1991–2009) have also been adapted for television several times in both Sweden and the UK, and the best-known Swedish version, starring Krister Henrikkson in the title role, is if anything even darker in tone than the books themselves. The popular image of Sweden is of an egalitarian-minded social democracy that compares very favourably in that respect to non-Scandinavian Europe, but the series as a whole does not present such a rosy picture. Relationships with the immigrant community can be very tense, for example, as they frequently are between generations too, and the other side of social democracy is a persistent undercurrent of neo-Nazi politics. It gives the impression of a society that is struggling to maintain its reputation for tolerance, and which is becoming far less content than it used to be – or thought it was anyway. There is a strong feeling of there being something very rotten in the state of Sweden: something which also comes through in Stieg Larsson's *Millennium Trilogy* (2005–7). The final series of *Wallander* becomes progressively gloomier, with Wallander fighting against the onset of Alzheimer's Disease, the signal that he too is fast approaching 'the worst of all'. The series spins the progress of the disease out over six episodes with different storylines, increasing the impact of the book it is based upon, *The Troubled Man*, which, with only one main plotline, telescoped the process.

Wallander sets out to show that when you dig under the surface of almost any society, you are likely to find some extremely unpleasant things happening there that can shake one's faith in human nature: crime fiction is essentially based on that premise. Greed, self-interest, cruelty and violence all abound, suggesting that civilized values may only form a thin veneer of our supposedly tolerant, liberal, democratic culture. Wallander's decline into Alzheimer's might almost be a metaphor for his country's apparent memory loss about its egalitarian past. The final episode where he tries to commit suicide but cannot bring himself to go through with the act is truly harrowing, although it could be read more positively as refusing to give in and carrying on despite knowing that the worst is already under way. Both Sartre and Camus would applaud that, and probably Beckett too.

The nastiness that lies under the surface of everyday life has also been a concern of the filmmaker David Lynch, and he has explored this topic in some particularly quirky works that express an essentially pessimistic outlook on the human condition. Lynch regards evil as a real presence in human affairs, and the protagonists of his films appear to be locked in an unequal battle with it as it repeatedly makes itself felt in their lives, threatening their sense of security. American small-town life in particular seems to seethe with an underlying sense of menace, for all its apparent everyday tranquillity, with greed, self-interest, cruelty and violence all being much in evidence. This is what we are to find in Lynch's cult television series *Twin Peaks* (1990–91), in which the local community is shaken to the core by the murder of a popular young woman. We are plunged into a network of interconnected events going back before the narrative's start, all revealing the hand of evil at work in the person of various human agents, whose outward manner can be disarmingly bland. You just cannot tell where the 'worst' will come from. The presence of evil is also signalled in somewhat startling fashion at the beginning of *Blue Velvet* (1986) when the protagonist comes across a severed human ear. Again, this is but the surface indication of an undercurrent of evil in society, suggesting that human nature cannot be trusted very far, and that its dark side is just waiting to assert itself. Lynch strikes you as someone well aware of its potential to do so. There is an oppressive feeling to his films, as if things might go wrong at any moment.

It is a menace that is always just out of his characters' grasp to counter effectively, and they labour under the strain of coping with it, much in the manner of Calvinist believers trying to come to terms with predestination. It is as if decisions have been already made about their fate, and despair and melancholy dog their lives. In *Inland Empire* (2006), for example, the protagonists are faced with a series of inexplicable events that they are ultimately unable to deal with, leaving them little better than emotional wrecks by the narrative's end, more or less in a state of limbo. The boundary between the characters' real and screen lives (they are making a film based on an earlier Polish film which was the subject of some tragic incidents) has blurred to the point where they barely know who or where they are any more. This does not suggest much optimism about human existence; anyone who dares to be optimistic in Lynch's world will soon be brought up short. The 'worst' is always just around the corner, just as it was in the novels of Thomas Hardy; the tenacity of evil means that you cannot escape encountering it at some point.

Another film to strike a note of resolute pessimism with regard to contemporary American life is *Nebraska*, directed by Alexander Payne and released in 2013. Set in a run-down and economically depressed American Midwest, the characters seem to bear out only too painfully the notion that we have little to look forward to but 'work, worry, toil and trouble'. Midwestern existence as they experience it appears to offer little else. They drift through life with no particular sense of direction or purpose, and the elderly, who make up a significant proportion of the small towns where the film's action occurs, are simply marking time before death arrives. The lead character, Woody Grant, is sinking into dementia and has a permanently frustrated air, aware somewhere in his mind that his life has not amounted to much and that death is all that is left. In the interim, his only escape is drinking. There is a general feeling among the film's characters that life has somehow passed them by, and judging by the shabby, deserted appearance of the towns where they reside, the same can probably be said for the entire region. Yet again we are being shown the other side of America, rather than the image it would prefer to project of itself as a rich and powerful nation, full of go-getters and a bright future. The empty streets and prairie landscapes echo the general emptiness of the lives of the inhabitants, as well as of the local economy. The stark black-and-white photography lends an appropriately sombre tone to the proceedings.

This is a world where most people distrust each other and at best are tolerating each others' company. There is a particularly joyless character to human relations, as if everyone is going through the motions and taking no pleasure in their daily round of activities; relationships are simply endured, with varying degrees of grace. Neither Woody nor his wife are contented with their marriage, and they bicker constantly; his son David's girlfriend has broken up with him and moved out; Woody's in-laws barely converse with each other, and mostly monosyllabically when they do. The younger generation is beginning to seem just as disillusioned with their prospects in life as the older generation has become with time, having been ground down by their long experience of boring routine. As one of Woody's in-laws puts it, life is hard in the area's towns for young men since the recession hit, and unemployment is widespread. With only the 'worry' and 'trouble' of Schopenhauer's sequence left remaining, it is a situation encouraging an increasingly bitter outlook. This is well exemplified by Woody's two nephews, who are stuck at home with their parents, without money or work, and have turned into mean and spiteful individuals with no sense of loyalty to their family. At one point they attack Woody and David in order to steal what turns out to be a worthless document. Previous to that, in every encounter with Woody and David they mock and insult them mercilessly, without any justification, showing no respect at all for their kin.

The document in question appears to say that Woody has won a million dollars, and he is obsessed with going to collect it from the town several hundred miles away where the company running the scheme is located. David attempts to dissuade him, telling him it is all a well-worn scam, but, worn down by his father's persistence, eventually gives in and drives him from Billings, Montana, over to Lincoln, Nebraska, and takes him to the offices of the company. Predictably, Woody is told that while his number was put forward for the million-dollar prize, it did not win; all the document really promises is that he has a (theoretical) chance of winning if his number happens to be the one that comes up. Woody's reaction on hearing this news is revealing; he does not argue the point and turns away with an air of resignation, as if he is so used to disappointment in his life that he now expects it as a matter of course. The system has defeated the little guy once more. Whether anyone ever does win is left very open to question, as is whether the million dollars actually exists anywhere to be won. Unlike Calvinist predestination, this may well be a lottery in which no-one ever hits the jackpot.

David enquires if others ever come to the company's office in search of their supposed winnings, and is told yes by the receptionist, and that it is usually old people like his father. In one of the most telling exchanges of the film, David replies that his father still believes what people tell him, to which the receptionist answers, 'That's too bad.' It would seem that you are expected to be sceptical, which reflects badly on the corporate sector and the lifestyle that has developed in con-temporary America. In a deeply ironic scene, the receptionist offers, and Woody fairly meekly accepts, a baseball-style cap with the phrase 'winner' emblazoned on it, as consolation for his unsuccessful journey in search of the supposed prize. Pictured wearing it in the car shortly afterwards, he cuts a sad figure, summing up the other side of the 'American dream', its promise of wealth and happiness for all not extending to him – or to anyone else in his circle either.

Although the film makes a gesture towards a slightly more upbeat ending, it could hardly be called optimistic. David indulges his father to the extent of making it appear that he has actually won the sought-after prize, so that he can impress his old acquaintances in the town near Lincoln where he grew up and where the in-laws they have been visiting still reside. All this amounts to is letting him drive down the town's main street in a truck he has bought in his father's name (buying a truck being the only reason Woody can specify for needing the prize money), so it is just an illusion of wealth. This, no matter how brief, is enough to keep reality at bay for his father, as well as the various acquaintances who gape at him as he drives down his home town's main street, as if that is the most that can be hoped for in modern America – not a message likely to dispel the air of pessimism hanging over the film. Life goes on, but the outlook is pretty grim in a nation looking anything like the 'land of opportunity' that it believes itself to be. For such as Woody and his class, it is more like a 'land of disappointment'.

War has also been well represented in film, and from Vietnam onwards films have become increasingly critical of the politics behind war and what this says about human nature. While it is still possible to make positive films about the Allied victory in the Second World War, and Hollywood continues to return to this subject, Vietnam and its successors comprise much more problematical material with which to work. Francis Ford Coppola's *Apocalypse Now* (1979), for example, is particularly successful at capturing the chaos of war and the effect it has on those caught up with it. Set in the Vietnam War, but taking inspiration from the storyline of Joseph Conrad's anti-colonial novel *Heart of Darkness* (1899), it offers a very pessimistic account of colonialism and imperialism, which are pictured as bringing out the very worst in human nature.

The inhumanity unleashed by war is emphasized very powerfully in Stanley Kubrick's *Paths of Glory* (1957) as well. The First World War is the setting this time around. The French general staff, safe in their headquarters away from the front line, have scant regard for the soldiers under their command, sending them on doomed attacks just to prove their 'heroism', turning them into mere fodder for propaganda campaigns to hide their side's failure to make significant progress in the conflict. When one group refuses to go on a suicidal attack, three of them are executed for disobeying orders.

The inhumanity that comes in the wake of war is also strongly conveyed in Oliver Stone's *Platoon* (1986), which draws on the director's own experience as a soldier in the Vietnam War. The character of Chris Taylor is based on Stone, and he is shocked by the conduct of his own comrades, who kill unarmed Vietnamese civilians when in a rage over the death of others in their platoon, subsequently turning on those who dare to voice objections. Sergeant Elias is one of the most vocal critics of the crime, and he is deliberately shot by one of the culprits when out on a jungle patrol in order to prevent him from revealing the truth of what happened, which might lead to charges being made against them. With memories of the My Lai massacre still fresh in American minds, the film is an indictment of war's brutalizing impact on everyone caught up in it.

Stone subsequently had plans to produce a documentary about My Lai until the studio backing it decided to pull out – mindful that it is still a very contentious topic in the country, and prone to provoke accusations of being unpatriotic. He has also directed two other films dealing with Vietnam (*Born on the Fourth of July* and *Heaven and Earth*): it is clearly not an issue he feels able to let lie.

Stone's film on the Kennedy assassination, *JFK* (1991), which posits a complex, high-level plot behind the event, is not optimistic either about what goes on in American domestic politics. How true the film is has to be open to question; conspiracy theories about the assassination have continued to be put forward regularly over the years, and always seem to find a ready audience. But the fact that Stone chose to present it in the form of a conspiracy, and an unsolved one at that, thanks to a large-scale cover-up that we must assume is still operating, does indicate someone with a pessimistic attitude towards his nation's political life. Stone has remained a resolute critic of American imperialism over his career, which he was also to attack in the film *Salvador* (1986), this time set in Latin America.

The most pessimistic aspect of films like these is that we know only too well from history that this is the way imperialist powers traditionally act. The West's more recent interventions in places like Iraq and Afghanistan do not suggest that very much has changed in this respect. The fact that the regime the allies set out to overthrow in Iraq was unquestionably tyrannical and inhuman does little to induce optimism about human nature: how does one choose between two such options, which merely point up the failings of human nature? How does one reach a position of optimism with regard to global politics? Less than complimentary films are already being produced about these episodes, and it is highly unlikely that we have seen the last of them. The situation in the Middle East alone is enough to indicate that there is every reason to be pessimistic about humanity's ability to resolve political disputes between different cultures, and to exemplify just how difficult we can find it to reach a compromise (which is not to say that we should stop trying, even if decades of this has resulted in precious little, if any, real progress being made). Jean-François Lyotard's concept of the 'differend' well describes what is involved in such situations; the opposed sides are operating from incompatible belief systems, rendering them unable to accept the validity of the other's past a certain point. But what does that tell us about humanity? Or about our prospects for significantly reducing the threat of violence and war? Pessimism invariably accompanies any serious contemplation of such issues.

Stone's two films about the stock market, *Wall Street* (1987) and *Wall Street: Money Never Sleeps* (2010), based on the exploits of the character Gordon Gekko, maintain the critical stance towards American institutions – as well as lodging Gekko's phrase that 'greed is good' in the public mind to represent everything that has gone wrong with the financial industry (as well as in the nation's morality). More recent efforts like Martin Scorsese's *The Wolf of Wall Street* (2013) do not suggest someone with a great deal of faith about how human nature operates in contemporary America, and as we know from Michael Lewis's *Flash Boys*, there is a wealth of damning evidence to back up such a view when it comes to its financial sector. The message that emerges from such films is that greed is anything but good, but how lasting an impact that is likely to have in a culture like America's, which makes such a fetish of wealth creation and the free market, remains to be seen. I would like to think it would, but scepticism accompanies such a hope.

* ✳ *

Much music sounds despondent and downbeat, which I concede is not the same thing as saying that it is the product of a pessimistic worldview. It might be an opera or a tone poem on a sad theme, and the composer may not generally choose a topic of that nature. Individual songs, too, may not always be characteristic of a composer's entire output, but merely geared to the poem they are setting. But some composers do seem to be expressing a pessimistic sensibility, as do certain musical styles, and I will analyse some of those in this section. We can go back as far in the modern period as the lute pieces of John Dowland, several of which seem to resonate with the melancholy that was becoming such a widespread cultural phenomenon in Elizabethan and Jacobean England (although Dowland's music can, admittedly, cover a variety of moods).

Gustav Mahler's work often has a distinctly sorrowful air, and this reaches a culmination in his Ninth – and last – Symphony. This was written when the composer was coming to terms with the implications of a serious heart complaint that was to lead to his death before the work was ever performed. The symphony is often interpreted as representing the composer's 'farewell to life', and although not all Mahler commentators agree with this reading, it does communicate a sense of resignation, even hopelessness, being suffused with feelings of melancholy. This is particularly true of the first movement, which slowly builds to a climax in the middle then collapses suddenly and dramatically, communicating a sense of the aftermath of a painful crisis, quite possibly one marking an irreversible turning point in one's experience, something that just has to be accepted no matter how difficult that may be (I have always thought of it, if this is not too fanciful, as akin to falling off a cliff). There is a funereal quality to much of the work that listeners can hardly miss. No-one hearing this is going to feel buoyed up by it, and it does sound very much like the work of someone confronting his very own doomsday clock.

Late Romanticism produced some notably melancholic music, with Sergei Rachmaninov being an example worth citing. Although he could write in an uplifting, even joyous manner on occasion, his minor-key melodies can have an ineffable sadness about them. Rachmaninov himself had a depressive personality, even experiencing a breakdown in his early career after the public failure of his First Symphony, and although one has to be careful about assuming that biographical details provide the key to any artwork's meaning (any more than in the case of Munch), much of his music sounds so downbeat that it does suggest a world viewed largely through that state of mind. His exile from Russia after the Revolution of 1917 did not help. There is always a certain amount of subjectivism involved in saying how a piece of music affects one emotionally, and your reaction may be very different from mine, but I would argue that listening to Rachmaninov is unlikely to make you feel more optimistic and upbeat about life. It is tailor-made to be the background to life's more sombre moments; music to make you reflect on the more wearying and care-inducing aspects of existence.

Much of Erik Satie's music sounds deeply melancholy as well, in particular probably his best-known piano work *Trois Gymnopédies*; a popular – to the point of cliché – choice among filmmakers and television producers to underscore emotionally dejecting episodes on screen (Rachmaninov has come in for his share of that treatment over the years, too). Satie's life was troubled in many ways. He was very much in the shadow of the more famous French composers of the day, Claude Debussy and Maurice Ravel, and he cut a lonely figure in Parisian life, leading a fairly straitened existence due to his lack of financial success. Again, I would venture to suggest that listening to, say, *Trois Gymnopédies* is unlikely to induce a feeling of optimism in you.

Dmitri Shostakovich's life was fraught with problems under the oppressive censorship operated by the Soviet regime, especially during Stalin's reign, and this comes through very powerfully in much of his music, which on occasion sounds quite desperate in tone. I am thinking particularly of the Fourth Symphony and the Fifteenth String Quartet. Although these works are not alone in his vast output in giving this impression, they are the ones that most obviously call attention to themselves. In both of them we sense a man at the end of his tether, aware that the worst was continuing to happen fairly relentlessly and that he is helpless as an individual to do anything about it – anything, that is, except suffer through it and express that in his art. In the two works mentioned, he does so rivetingly.

The Fourth Symphony has been interpreted as a portrait of Stalin, illustrating all his tyrannical qualities, which were becoming steadily more apparent by the 1930s (see particularly Ian MacDonald's book *The New Shostakovich* on this[17]). These qualities were coming to a head in the notorious purges of opponents over the course of the decade, involving forced confessions and effectively silencing any potential opposition to Stalin from other important figures in the party, many of whom were considered up until then to be heroes of the Revolution and the Bolshevik triumph. Shostakovich himself lived in almost permanent fear of arrest in what was clearly turning into a brutal police state under Stalin's iron rule, and he was the victim of censorship at various times in his life for writing music considered by the authorities to be decadent and degenerate, far too harsh and dissonant for the standards laid down for Soviet artists. Soviet artists were expected to produce work that pointed towards a bright new future for the people under communist leadership, and that is not something that can be said of Shostakovich at this point in his career. The optimism that marked out the early days of the Soviet system, and is evident in Shostakovich's own early compositions (his First Symphony, for example), is being emphatically rejected as false. The aesthetic doctrine of socialist realism was promoted enthusiastically by the authorities; Stalin had even appointed a Commissar for the Arts, the dreaded A. A. Zhdanov, who terrorized the lives of the Soviet creative community in the name of Socialist Realism. The doctrine did not allow for music as discordant as Shostakovich's Fourth turned out to be, and publicly condemned anyone who did not follow its line. The result, as critics of the system like Bertolt Brecht had already pointed out would happen in literature, was work that sounded out of date, as the compositions of most of Shostakovich's contemporaries were rapidly becoming in response to the threat of censorship – or worse.

Shostakovich himself soon felt compelled to follow the same route as his cowed contemporaries, presenting his much more traditional Fifth Symphony as his 'apology' to the Soviet public for his recent 'mistakes'. His works from then onwards are thought to be coded, containing expressions of internal self-assertion that only the composer could recognize, defying the authorities' treatment of him. These were largely successful in hiding his true feelings about his own situation behind an apparently conformist style. He may have been lauded by the authorities at his death in 1975, and given a state funeral with all the trappings, but afterwards a very different picture of Shostakovich gradually began to emerge, in which he 'turned out to have been a secret dissident waging, from behind the many masks of his music, a campaign of protest against the very system which had paraded him as its laureate'.[18] His friend the conductor Mstislav Rostropovich has insisted that we should not be taken in by the Fifth Symphony's 'apology', and especially the apparent optimism of its last movement: 'anyone who thinks the finale is glorification is an idiot'.[19]

There was precious little to be optimistic about in Russia during the period in which the Fourth Symphony was written, with Stalin's tightening grip on power provoking fear and terror among the populace. No-one could really feel safe from hearing the dreaded 'knock on the door' that announced the arrival of the secret police. A work of Shostakovich's completed just before the symphony, the opera *Lady Macbeth of the Mtsensk District*, was savagely attacked in the Communist Party newspaper *Pravda* after a performance of it attended by Stalin and other party notables, in an article (very likely written by Stalin) entitled 'Muddle instead of Music'. The *Pravda* piece even warned Shostakovich to beware of coming to a bad end if he was to be foolish enough to go on in the same vein. *Lady Macbeth* subsequently disappeared from the Soviet repertoire, to be revived only after Stalin's death, and it is now recognized as one of the composer's most striking and original scores.

Although the Fourth Symphony was written in 1935–6, it was not performed publicly in Russia until 1961, several years after Stalin's death. It is a disturbing work, highly evocative of the social and political turmoil of the age. It explodes at one point near the end in what can only be defined as an outburst of rage, a cry of utter frustration at the way Soviet society was developing and what it was doing to its citizens. The entire symphony has an edgy quality that is deeply unsettling, and it is not surprising that Shostakovich felt it prudent to withdraw the work from rehearsal before its scheduled remiere in Leningrad in 1936. Listening to it now, it comes across as a very subversive piece of music, the exact antithesis of the conformist character of so much of what was being produced (under duress, as we now know) by Soviet creative artists of the time trying to meet the requirements of Socialist Realism. Given the prevailing suspicion of him in the top circles of the party, it could well have led to his imprisonment if the performance had gone ahead as planned. It does make one wonder, as does *Lady Macbeth of the Mtsensk District*, how Shostakovich might have developed as a composer under a less oppressive regime. A pessimistic outlook on existence is only too understandable for someone trapped within a system like the Soviet one, which in retrospect appears as yet another tragedy to befall the Russian people, following on from the repression and violence of the nineteenth-century Czarist regime. Shostakovich fits into a tradition of pessimism running back to figures from that earlier era such as Dostoevsky.

Occasionally, Shostakovich and the Stalinist regime could reach an accommodation on objectives, as in his Seventh, or 'Leningrad', Symphony, written as an act of defiance to the German siege of the city, which was Shostakovich's home. This stirring work, performed in Leningrad by a small orchestra of starving musicians during the bombardment, was broadcast to the Russian people and used as a propaganda weapon by the Soviet government – who even broadcast it out at the German troops camped around the city. Shostakovich's Eighth

String Quartet was written at the end of the war as a memorial 'to the victims of fascism and war'. It is yet another emotionally moving composition, expressing the composer's pain at the turbulent times he has been living through, from the reign of terror in the 1930s to the appalling losses suffered by Russia in the war against fascism – twenty million dead, it has been estimated.

The Fifteenth String Quartet is a much later work, written towards the end of the composer's life, and it is one of the most depressing pieces to be found in twentieth-century music, saturated with an air of almost suicidal-sounding despair. Optimism about the prospects for humanity would be difficult to muster after listening to this grim piece, which makes full use of the melancholic effect of minor keys. Downbeat is not adequate to describe the impression it leaves. It is the work of a man whose entire life experience has encouraged a pessimistic response, and who is not about to pretend otherwise. Even though the Soviet regime had loosened up somewhat since the days of Stalinism, Shostakovich does not sound convinced that it will bring about the brave new world that communism had promised in its early days. Film of him taken in his last years reveals a very dejected-looking individual, a man weighed down by the cares of the world: pessimism by then seems to have become entrenched in his being.

Another particularly painful-sounding work from the Second World War period worth mentioning in this context is Olivier Messiaen's *Quartet for the End of Time*, written during his internment in a prisoner of war camp in 1941. France had been swamped by the invading German army and the future looked distinctly unpromising, with a Nazi victory seeming the likeliest outcome at the time. The quartet's first performance took place in the camp, with the only four musicians and instruments available there, including Messiaen himself on piano. Full of Messiaen's characteristically jagged rhythms and dissonant harmonies, it is a work that communicates despair and foreboding at the state of the world, and sadness at the prospects for humankind.

War has affected other modern composers, notably Michael Tippett and Benjamin Britten. Tippett's oratorio *A Child of Our Time*, which was completed during the Second World War, was composed in memory of the events surrounding the Nazi pogrom Kristallnacht in 1938, which was unleashed as punishment for the death of a German diplomat at the hands of a Jewish refugee in Paris. Kristallnacht signalled to the world the depth of hatred and cruelty that lay behind the Nazi campaign against the Jews that was to culminate in the Holocaust. Britten's *War Requiem* of 1961 included settings of poems from the First World War by Wilfred Owen, providing a reminder of just how war-torn the twentieth century had been. Both men were well known for their anti-war views, and were conscientious objectors to the Second World War at a time when this was a distinctly unpopular stance to adopt in Britain: Tippett was even imprisoned briefly.

The music that emerged out of German Expressionism has a decidedly tortured quality to it, suggesting a pessimistic sensibility, for all the apparent optimism of composers like Arnold Schoenberg that they had discovered a completely new sound world through the method of serialism (or 'twelve-tone' composition). That is undoubtedly correct: there had not been anything quite like it in Western culture before. But that sound world did tend to be used by its earliest exponents in the service of themes and materials dealing with the dark side of human nature, reminding us that it was the product of a Viennese culture where psychoanalysis was establishing itself under the leadership of Sigmund Freud.

Freud is often described as a pessimist on the basis of what his theories claim about humanity. From his perspective, we are not really in control of our inner drives and instincts, most of which are hidden away in our subconscious and are often in direct opposition to how we are trying to behave in our conscious world. Even more worryingly, no matter how much we attempt to suppress these often anti-social drives and instincts (*very* anti-social by the standards of the Viennese culture of the time), they will break out eventually in what Freud terms 'the return of the repressed', merely confirming the notion that we are to a large extent at the mercy of things inside us that we cannot understand.[20] There is no absolute power on the Hobbesian model to keep our instincts permanently in check.

Serialism was developed by the 'Second Viennese School', comprising Schoenberg and his pupils Alban Berg and Anton Webern. The first two had a distinct preference for dark and depressing themes in their work. Berg's operas *Wozzeck* and *Lulu* are deeply gloomy, the former being based on an equally gloomy play, *Woyzeck*, left unfinished by the nineteenth-century German dramatist Georg Büchner. The protagonist, a lowly soldier, is being used in a dubious-sounding dietary experiment by a local doctor, which may be unsettling his mind if his bad dreams are anything to go by. He ends up murdering his lover, Marie, when he discovers that she has been unfaithful to him with another soldier, a local drum major. In an attempt to retrieve the knife with which he has stabbed Marie to death, Wozzeck drowns in the pool where he had thrown it earlier. In the last scene, their now-orphaned child is left alone on stage as a crowd rushes off to view Marie's newly discovered corpse.

The opera's music is extremely dissonant, as befits such a sensationalist tale, and to ears accustomed to the more traditional Western style of tonal harmony, as most of the public is, that is what serial composition almost always sounds like. Serial music has now gone largely out of fashion among composers, never really having caught on to any great extent among the general music-listening public (even today it is considered risky programming by most concert promoters).

It is a method only too well suited to communicating angst and emotional trauma, and that did prove to be very much the forte of both Berg and Schoenberg.

Lulu is a setting of two plays by the Austrian dramatist Frank Wedekind (*Earth Spirit* and *Pandora's Box*), about a beautiful dancer who embarks on a series of sexual relationships with rich and powerful men, eventually sinking into a life of prostitution and then death in London at the hands of Jack the Ripper. Lulu is seen as a symbol of both the power and the destructiveness of female sexuality, and the opera constitutes something of a warning as to what can happen when this is given free rein. Again, the music is notably harsh in tone, designed to capture the atmosphere of a narrative that is as lurid and ultimately depressing in its effect as *Wozzeck*. Human nature does not come out very well from either tale, being only too prone to exploitation and the creation of victims – especially when it involves sexual matters.

Berg's Violin Concerto is yet another very downbeat work. It was written 'in memory of an angel', a friend's young daughter who had died of polio. The overall tone ranges from the anguished to the mournful. It is a sustained meditation on death and the transience of human existence. Once again, it is not likely to induce positive feelings in the listener; it is far more likely to leave you in low spirits.

Schoenberg, too, is drawn to melodramatic themes and plots in which characters have to cope with mysterious forces they can barely understand. *Moses and Aaron* provides a telling example of this. It is an unfinished opera based on biblical material, featuring the character of Moses grappling with powers apparently beyond his control. There is God on the one hand, insisting that he must deliver the Ten Commandments to his chosen people in order to make them renounce their pagan ways, and the unruly Israelites Moses is leading out of captivity in Egypt on the other. When the Israelites revert to their old religion of worshipping the golden calf in the temporary absence of Moses, their behaviour declines into an anarchic shedding of their inhibitions (a recent production by Welsh National Opera emphasized the sexual aspect of this, which seems entirely appropriate to Schoenberg's Viennese intellectual background). The work's specifically Jewish themes mark out a return to his roots by the composer, who, despite having converted to Christianity at an early point in his life, nevertheless became a victim of anti-Semitism in an era which saw the dramatic rise of fascism in the German-speaking world. Like many of his Jewish compatriots, Schoenberg fled this milieu as the situation grew steadily worse, settling in America. However, a sense of pessimism was almost guaranteed to be induced in anyone who had gone through such an experience and had had to observe the worst side of human nature asserting itself to such disastrous effect. Settling in Hollywood, as Schoenberg did, would not do much to dissuade you of taking a pessimistic view of human nature either, one imagines.

Schoenberg's most important early composition (and probably still his best-known) is *Pierrot Lunaire*, one of the most powerful works of the Expressionist style. It contains wild changes of mood and angular, grating harmonies unlike anything else heard in classical music up to that point. It is a setting for a small chamber group and singer of poems by the French poet Albert Giraud. The poems feature a 'moonstruck' harlequin figure (the singer being dressed in that fashion) delivering a series of vignettes full of grotesque images – a gallows, crucifixion and so on – in a highly melodramatic fashion. The singer is required to perform the text in *Sprechtstimme* ('speech-singing'), a method pitched somewhere between singing and speaking that taxes the performer considerably. It still sounds very odd to this day, an unsettling, otherworldly work.

* ❋ *

The blues is a musical genre that is steeped in pessimism, displaying a jaundiced view on life from the perspective of a social group that suffers systematic discrimination on a daily basis. Blues is now a fairly loose term adapted by various musical styles such as jazz, rock and pop, and it soon drew input from white songwriters and performers, but in its early days it was the music of the African American community and expressed the trials and tribulations of their downtrodden status within the USA's culture (it was often referred to in its earlier days, revealingly enough, as 'race music'). Its themes are elemental: poverty, hardship, maltreatment, mean employers, death, oppression, injustice, alcoholism, untrue friends, untrustworthy lovers – all the things that would make you truly pessimistic about your lot in life. As a consequence, it often sounds very mournful (as one aging bluesman tartly commented at a rock festival on the spectacle of white blues bands playing in an upbeat manner, 'the blues don't need no jumpin'). These are quintessentially songs about 'work, worry, toil and trouble', and the painful realization that life is unlikely to get much better for the singer or his or her peers. The Lightnin' Slim song 'Bad Luck Blues' (1954), complains that bad luck seems to be the only kind of luck the singer ever knows (the notion of bad luck is recurrent in the genre). It is life as a vale of tears with only brief moments of respite, and those will generally come at a cost somewhere down the line (and probably sooner rather than later). The human condition is something to be endured rather than celebrated.

The song that more than any other established blues within the public consciousness was W. C. Handy's 'St Louis Blues' (1914), which begins with a typical expression of lament about having to face the night all alone. This is a tale of loss, the loss of one's lover who has deserted you for another, and it has become a jazz staple, both as a song and a straight instrumental. 'St James Infirmary' is an even sadder blues song from the early days of jazz.[21] Originally a folk song, it was subsequently adapted and altered over the years and exists in various versions, but it became popular after a famous recording of it by Louis Armstrong in 1928. Its morbid lyrics deal with death and loss, the singer recounting a trip to the morgue to identify a lover's corpse, and being shocked at the sight of the body lying lifeless on a slab there; a stark tale with stark imagery, manifestly a 'vision of despair'.

'Strange Fruit', written in 1937 by Abel Meeropol, a white Jewish teacher from New York (who was also a communist), as an attack on the racism so entrenched in American culture, is transformed into an example of blues at its most haunting in the version sung by the jazz great Billie Holliday in 1939. The subject of the song is lynching – a practice that was only too common an event in the American South of the early twentieth century, in the heyday of the Ku Klux Klan. It is difficult not to become pessimistic about human nature when contemplating such phenomena from what is not all that long ago in the past. Oppression and injustice could hardly be communicated more poignantly than they are here, with the images of African American bodies hanging on trees like 'strange fruit', and Holliday's voice wrings all the desperate sadness it can out of the song. The blues at such points becomes a historical record of bad times.

Soul music takes over something of the spirit of the blues tradition, although it is an avowedly more commercial genre. It is full of tales of the hardships of African American life, such as having to deal with discrimination, prejudice and poverty, and the sheer grind of daily life at the bottom of the social pile. Marvin Gaye's album *What's Going On* of 1971 is an impassioned commentary on the recent race riots in the 1960s and '70s, which left cities like Detroit as ruined shells. Detroit has never really recovered from the experience, with large areas of the city now deserted, much of the housing derelict and the population less than half of what it was before the riots. There is a particular poignancy to the song, as

Detroit was the home of the leading soul record label of the time, Motown, which soon afterwards deserted the city to move to Los Angeles. It was a symbol of African American pride and self-assertion, and Gaye was one of the label's most prominent stars.

It is possible to argue that rap music has carried on some of the traditions of blues and soul, although what was so often resignation in the latter has turned into anger about the situation of African Americans in the USA – particularly regarding relations between the African American community and the police. The sentiments expressed in such numbers are extremely pessimistic about the motives of the police (as well as often revenge-oriented in how to react to these, sometimes calling for officers to be attacked or killed), and about any possibility of significant change in what the performers take to be entrenched anti-African American attitudes among this mainly white organization.

Rap started out as a protest movement, and an unashamedly provocative and angry one at that (as in the Los Angeles group Niggaz With Attitude (NWA)). It was the voice of young urban male youth, right down to the rather depressing, often misogynistically inclined views on gender. But like any other form of music that becomes popular in America, it has since fallen prey to commercialism and is not always as political as it initially was. At first it really did seem to encapsulate the general distrust and pessimism found in the African American community regarding the promises of politicians in a white-dominated country. I confess that I find rap more interesting sociologically than musically, but no doubt others will choose to differ. Whatever the verdict, it may well come in time to constitute an important historical record, as does the blues.

For all their differences, country and western music springs from a similar social situation to the blues, this time from the poor white community in the American South. Again, its themes are frequently the hardship of life and how easy it can be for the individual to go under: love goes wrong, your marriage breaks up, you lose your job, alcohol wrecks your life, death strikes the family – the familiar story of lives at the bottom end of society (although of course not quite as low or disadvantaged as their poor African American neighbours). Country and western is now an industry that has moved a long way from its roots, and it can be almost a caricature of itself a lot of the time, all tacky glamour and false sentiment (you can probably tell that I am not much of a fan). These days it is mostly determinedly commercial, but at its best its lyrics adopt a stoic attitude towards life and its many troubles, that is tinged with a pessimism not unlike that found in the blues (in a style dubbed 'New Country', some younger performers have revived something of the spirit and themes of the genre's roots). Using country and western is another favourite way in which film-makers point up melancholic moments. 'Work, worry, toil and trouble' just have to be faced up to: that is the human condition, which is especially keenly felt by the ordinary man and woman who struggle to make ends meet in what can be a ruthless and uncaring society that is geared to success rather than failure. The best outcome only rarely arrives here.

Despair about men and their sexual mores comes across very powerfully in one of country and western's most famous songs, 'It Wasn't God Who Made Honky Tonk Angels', recorded by Kitty Wells in 1952 and by many other female artists since (although intriguingly enough, it was written by a male songwriter, J. D. Miller). It was a response to Hank Thompson's 1952 hit 'The Wild Side of Life', complaining about the singer's bride-to-be running off with a man she had met in a roadhouse bar (or 'honky tonk' as they were collo-quially known), and wondering why God had made women like that. The responding song, using the same tune as Thompson's, strongly denied that the blame lay with God, laying it squarely on the shoulders of philandering men who led women astray by pretending they were still single when they were really married. There is a world-weary pessimism about men and male morality being expressed here, in sentiments with which any modern-day feminist could readily sympathize. These situations occur all the time in a patriarchal culture, where women are treated as inferior beings, and men are left free to make them into 'honky tonk angels' with very little in the way of condemnation of their own conduct. One could almost regard this as a rueful acknowledgement of biological essentialism: the male is the predator, the female just the unfortunate victim. It could, however, be considered a redeeming feature that the writer is male, thus preserving the pessimist's belief that the worst will almost always happen – but only 'almost'.

* ✳ *

Literature, painting, music – the creative arts yield a host of visions of despair, all providing reasons enough to be pessimistic about human nature and wary of its dark side asserting itself. By engaging with such material, we gain a greater understanding of the complexity both of our nature and the world around us. The limitations of optimism need to be identified, and that is what we find happening in the work of the assorted writers, artists, film-makers and composers discussed in these last two chapters. They are not about to pretend that it is possible to avoid the many problems posed by 'work, worry, toil and trouble', or that we can lead charmed lives, nor to ignore the fact that war, violence, crime, greed and evil actions continue to blight the lives of many, and to cast doubt on the depth of our culture's humanitarian pretensions. What they present us with is a record of what Philip Roth refers to as 'the human stain': where we have failed, where we have done something indefensible we find difficult to live with afterwards, where we have exploited others, where we have ceased to cope with events. And that is a record of which we should all be aware.

SEVEN

The Benefits of a Half-empty Glass: Pessimism as a Lifestyle

Our tour through history has identified a multitude of reasons to be pessimistic, reasons that are still very pertinent today and cannot simply be dismissed as a lack of daring. For a host of thinkers and creative artists – and although we have considered quite a few here, many more could be cited – pessimism is the logical attitude to adopt about the human condition. Yet there is no need to consider this conclusion depressing. On the contrary, I consider it to be a realistic one that gives due weight to the catalogue of evidence available to us, providing an antidote to optimism – especially that propounded by such zealots as the neo-liberal brigade, with their uncritical commitment to 'growthism' as the answer to all our problems. It is not necessary to sink into despondency and gloom if one takes up this perspective. Yes, Schopenhauer does, but his version of pessimism is not the whole story. Like any other 'ism', pessimism is open to a variety of interpretations, running from Schopenhauer's right through to Robert Burton's 'good-humoured' variety and the 'chearfullest resignation' of Francis Burney's fictional heroine Cecilia, someone for whom the glass clearly is half-empty. Accepting that it is half-empty prepares you better for what the future may hold.

I regard pessimism as acknowledging what the reality of human nature can be like, especially if it is given free rein, and as admitting the many things about the world, including the complex mechanisms of physical nature, over which we can never exercise total control – remember the Aral Sea. Perhaps above all it recognizes that our daring has limits. Optimism has to be balanced by pessimism to give a true picture of our existence. It would be naive to expect the best outcome to keep on arriving just because that suits us better: the world just does not work that way. This may induce feelings of anxiety, as it clearly does in existentialists, but that is a perfectly natural reaction to have to a situation that runs counter to the desire to dominate that our culture has encouraged so enthusiastically in the modern age. I may not go along with Schopenhauer's assertion that it is an 'inborn error' to believe 'that we exist in order to be happy', but I do believe that it is one to think, as Leibniz did, that we live in 'the best of all possible worlds'.[1] The best of all possible worlds to a neo-liberal economist is certainly not mine.

That this seems a long way from being the best of all possible worlds is the message that has emerged from the various texts, belief systems and debates that have been surveyed in this book, and as I stated at the beginning, these are only a sample of what may be called the discourse of pessimism. Fictional literature, film, art and music collectively constitute a particularly rich source of material, and could yield many more examples than are presented here (I am sure any reader could come up with his or her own list of candidates[2]). Creative artists have an acute sensitivity to what Hamlet referred to as 'The heart-ache and the thousand natural shocks / That flesh is heir to' (Act III, Scene i), and no doubt they will continue to pass on their findings in their work. There is no denying that pessimism has left its mark on our cultural history, and rather than rejecting it outright as wrong-headed (the Ridley response), or even as an unfortunate pathological state that one should strive to banish from one's mind, we should pay far more attention to why this has turned out to be so. It is by no means unnatural to be a pessimist, not with phenomena like climate change to contemplate, or the various wars that humanity in general appears to be 'heir to'. It has to be recognized that there isn't always a 'bright side'.

I have argued that pessimism is an eminently justifiable attitude to embrace when we consider all the evidence to hand, a very necessary counter to the blithe assumption of optimism about the likely course of human affairs. There are a good many reasons to take a pessimistic attitude towards life, and starting from the premise that the glass is half-empty seems only sensible. But it is worth reiterating the point made consistently throughout this survey that being pessimistic about likely outcomes does not mean giving up and resigning oneself to fate. 'Fail again, fail better' may not be a plausible candidate for a political slogan, but it will work fine as a guiding principle for pessimists – just as long as you think very carefully about what it is that you are choosing to fail better at. Failing better at some madcap geoengineering scheme undertaken in a spirit of blinkered optimism would hardly qualify, especially if the initial failure had made things radically worse than they were beforehand by having the opposite effect to the one intended. Grand schemes of this nature should always be treated with considerable scepticism, and to be fair, they generally are by scientists.

Pessimists may well display a sense of cynicism on occasion about certain projected courses of action, but never fatalism, not even when the worst happens yet again. They must first work out what that worst might be and whether it should be left in the hands of the optimists, who really do have to be countered, and repeatedly so. Better to reduce consumption, one would think, than to cover large parts of the Earth with white sheeting, fill the oceans with iron, or fire 55,000 mirrors out into deep space and hope you have got it right. Why not fail better at trying to achieve such a reduction rather than going ahead with any of the latter courses of action – to the dismay of the profit-hungry manufacturers of the products in question?

The point in such cases as geoengineering schemes, no matter how hypothetical they may be at this stage in the global warming process, is that someone has to express the downside and ask what the contingency plans are if the expected outcome does not arrive. Pessimists would regard this as a social duty rather than just being miserable for the sake of it (a criticism you have to become used to hearing as a pessimist, I am afraid). The same goes for any grandiose scheme: they always sound exciting, and that can affect people's judgement, making the sceptical pessimist on the sidelines all the more necessary. This is especially true when companies start eyeing new sources of profit, which has a depressing tendency to drown out other arguments in the name of supposedly all-conquering 'growthism'. Pessimists do tend to dwell on downsides – that goes with their territory – but sometimes being a killjoy is the right and proper thing to do.

Pessimism can be more reactive than it is generally thought to be, therefore, and that is what I recommend we should aim for: dare to be a pessimist.

REFERENCES

ONE The Glass is Always Half-full? Countering the Optimists

1 Roger Scruton, *The Uses of Pessimism and the Danger of False Hope* (Oxford, 2010), pp. 22–3.

2 Matt Ridley, *The Rational Optimist: How Prosperity Evolves* (London, 2010), p. 359.

3 Ibid., p. 12.

4 Ibid., p. 15.

5 Zygmunt Bauman, *Intimations of Postmodernity* (London, 1992), p. 179.

6 James Lovelock, *The Revenge of Gaia: Earth's Climate Crisis and the Fate of Humanity* (London, 2006).

7 Joshua Foa Dienstag, *Pessimism: Philosophy, Ethic, Spirit* (Princeton, NJ, 2006), p. xi.

8 I discuss these ideas in more detail in chapter Nine of my book *The Carbon Footprint Wars: What Might Happen If We Retreat from Globalization?* (Edinburgh, 2009).

9 For more on my views on this topic, see my book *Addicted to Profit: Reclaiming Our Lives From the Free Market* (Edinburgh, 2012).

10 Ian Morris, *War! What Is It Good For? The Role of Conflict in Civilisation, from Primates to Robots* (London, 2014), p. 9.

11 See Clemens Hetschko, Andreas Knabe, and Ronnie Schöb, 'Changing Identity: Retiring From Unemployment', *Economic Journal*, CXXIV/575 (2014), pp. 149–66.

two The 'Doomsday Clock' is Always with Us:
Pessimism in History

1 John Calvin, *Institutes of the Christian Religion* [1536], I–II, trans. Ford Lewis Battles (London, 1961), II, p. 937.
2 Ibid., II, p. 957.
3 John Bunyan, *Grace Abounding to the Chief of Sinners* [1666], ed. W. R. Owens (Harmondsworth, 1987), p. 26.
4 Ibid., p. 27.
5 Ibid., p. 59.
6 Ibid., p. 73.
7 John Bunyan, *The Life and Death of Mr Badman* [1680], ed. James F. Forrest and Roger Sharrock (Oxford, 1988), p. 157.
8 John Bunyan, *The Pilgrim's Progress* [1678], ed. W. R. Owens (Oxford, 2003), p. 34.
9 Ibid., p. 154.
10 Daniel Defoe, *The Life and Strange Surprising Adventures of Robinson Crusoe* [1719], ed. Thomas Keymer (Oxford, 2007), pp. 82–3.
11 Daniel Defoe, *A Journal of the Plague Year* [1722], ed. Louis Landa (London, 1969), p. 11.
12 Ibid., p. 33.
13 Daniel Defoe, *Roxana: The Fortunate Mistress* [1724], ed. John Mullan (Oxford, 1996), p. 330.
14 James Hogg, *The Private Memoirs and Confessions of a Justified Sinner* [1824], ed. John Carey (Oxford, 1981), p. 2.
15 Ibid., p. 122.
16 Ibid., p. 132.
17 Ibid., p. 240.
18 Hilary Mantel, *Eight Months on Ghazzah Street* [1988] (London, 2013), pp. 85–6.
19 *The Koran*, trans. N. J. Dawood (Harmondsworth, 1974), p. 72.
20 Ibid., p. 109.
21 Andrew Marvell, 'To His Coy Mistress', in *The Metaphysical Poets*, ed. Helen Gardner (Harmondsworth, 1966), p. 250.
22 George Herbert, 'Vertue', ibid., p. 127.
23 John Donne, 'A Nocturnal upon St Lucie's day, Being the Shortest Day', ibid., p. 71.
24 Lisa Grossman, 'Quantum Twist Could Kill Off the Multiverse', *New Scientist*, 14 May 2014, pp. 8–9 (p. 8).

25 Ibid., p. 9.

26 Benoit Mandelbrot, *Fractals and Scaling in Finance: Discontinuity, Concentration, Risk* (New York, 1997), p. 471.

27 Holbrook Jackson, 'Introduction' to Robert Burton, *The Anatomy of Melancholy* (London, 1932), p. v.

28 Burton, 'The First Partition', in *The Anatomy of Melancholy*, p. 171.

29 George Cheyne, *The English Malady: or, A Treatise of Nervous Diseases of all Kinds*, ed. Roy Porter (London, 1991).

30 Bunyan, *Grace Abounding to the Chief of Sinners*, p. 37.

31 Allan Ingram, 'Deciphering Difference: A Study in Medical Literacy', in *Melancholy Experience in the Literature of the Long Eighteenth Century*, ed. Allan Ingram et al. (Basingstoke, 2011), pp. 170–202 (p. 181).

32 Clark Lawlor, 'Fashionable Melancholy', in *Melancholy Experience in the Literature of the Long Eighteenth Century*, ed. Ingram et al., pp. 25–53 (p. 25).

33 Henry Fielding, *Miscellanies*, in *The Wesleyan Edition of the Works of Henry Fielding*, I–III, ed. Henry Knight Miller (Oxford 1967), I, p. 224.

34 Theodor W. Adorno, *Prisms*, trans. Samuel and Shierry Weber (Cambridge, MA, 1981), p. 34.

35 *The Koran*, p. 105.

36 Tom Stoppard, *Jumpers* (London, 1986), p. 78.

37 See G. W. Leibniz, *The Monadology and Other Philosophical Writings*, trans. Robert Latta (London, 1971), p. 345.

38 William Godwin, *Enquiry Concerning Political Justice*, ed. Isaac Kramnick (London, 1985), p. 554.

39 Karl Marx, *Critique of the Gotha Programme* [1875], in Karl Marx and Frederick Engels, *Selected Works* (London, 1968), p. 325.

40 Mark Cowling, 'Can Marxism Make Sense of Crime?', in *The Legacy of Marxism: Contemporary Challenges, Conflicts and Developments*, ed. Matthew Johnson (London and New York, 2012), pp. 135–47 (p. 139).

41 Hans J. Eysenck, *Race, Intelligence and Education* (London, 1971), p. 130.

42 Hélène Cixous, 'The Laugh of the Medusa', in *New French Feminisms*, ed. Elaine Marks and Isabelle de Courtivron (Brighton, 1981), pp. 245–64 (pp. 245, 247).

43 Luce Irigaray, *This Sex Which Is Not One*, trans. Catherine Porter, with Carolyn Burke (Ithaca, NY, 1985), p. 29.

44 Ibid., p. 25.

45 Luce Irigaray, *Je, Tu, Nous: Towards a Culture of Sexual Difference*, trans. Alison Martin (New York and London, 1993), p. 6.

46 Monique Wittig, *Les Guérillères*, trans. David Le Vay (New York, 1973), pp. 102–3.

47 Francis Burney, *Cecilia* [1782], ed. Margaret Anne Doody and Peter Sabor (Oxford, 1988), p. 941.

48 Ibid.

49 Claude Lévi-Strauss, *The Raw and the Cooked*, trans. J. and D. Weightman (London, 1969), p. 147.

50 Roland Barthes, *Image Music Text*, trans. Stephen Heath (London, 1977), p. 143.

51 Ibid.

THREE Optimists v. Pessimists: Economics and Politics

1 For de-growth theory, see Serge Latouche, *Farewell to Growth*, trans. David Macey (Cambridge and Malden, MA, 2009).

2 See Charles B. Kindleberger, *Manias, Panics, and Crashes: A History of Financial Crises* (London and Basingstoke, 1978).

3 Michael Lewis, *Flash Boys: Cracking the Money Code* (London, 2014), p. 3.

4 Latouche, *Farewell to Growth*, p. 2.

5 Lewis, *Flash Boys*, p. 266.

6 For other critical investigations of the system, see Paul Krugman, *The Return of Depression Economics and the Crisis of 2008* (London, 2008); Graham Turner, *The Credit Crunch: Housing Bubbles, Globalisation and the Worldwide Economic Crisis* (London, 2008); Gillian Tett, *Fool's Gold: How Unrestrained Greed Corrupted a Dream, Shattered Global Markets and Unleashed a Catastrophe* (London, 2009); and Philip Augar, *Chasing Alpha: How Reckless Growth and Unchecked Ambition Ruined the City's Golden Decade* (London, 2009). This is only a sample, however, of what is on the way to becoming almost a sub-genre in its own right.

7 Lewis, *Flash Boys*, p. 232.

8 Ibid., p. 18.

9 Naomi Klein, *No Logo* (London, 2001).

10 Guy Standing, *The Precariat: The New Dangerous Class* (London, 2011), and *A Precariat Charter: From Denizens to Citizens* (London, 2014).

11 Georg Lukács, *Political Writings, 1919–1929*, trans. Michael McColgan, ed. Rodney Livingstone (London 1972), p. 101.

12 Thomas Piketty, *Capital in the Twenty-first Century*, trans. Arthur Goldhammer (Cambridge, MA, 2014), p. 1.

13 Ibid., p. 6.

14 Milton Friedman, *Capitalism and Freedom*, 2nd edn [1962] (Chicago, IL, and London, 1982), p. 133.

15 See Matt Wells, 'Paxman Answers the Questions', www.theguardian.com, accessed 5 May 2014.

16 'Pass Notes: Is Joni Ernst the New Sarah Palin?', *The Guardian*, G2 Section (21 May 2014), p. 3.

FOUR I Think, Therefore I Expect the Worst: Pessimism in Philosophy

1 René Descartes, *Philosophical Writings*, trans. and ed. Elizabeth Anscombe and Peter Thomas Geach (London, 1970), p. 67.

2 Sextus Empiricus, *Outlines of Scepticism*, trans. Julia Annas and Jonathan Barnes (Cambridge, 1994), p. 72.

3 Ibid., p. 216.

4 Ibid., p. 4.

5 David Hume, *Enquiries Concerning Human Understanding and Concerning the Principles of Morals* [1748], 3rd edn, ed. P. H. Nidditch (Oxford, 1975), p. 43.

6 Ludwig Wittgenstein, *Tractatus Logico-Philosophicus* [1921], trans. D. F. Pears and B. F. McGuinness (London and Henley, 1961), p. 70.

7 Thomas Hobbes, *Leviathan, or, The Matter, Forme, and Power of a Free Common-Wealth Ecclesiasticall and Civill* [1651], ed. C. B. Macpherson (Harmondsworth, 1968), p. 189.

8 Ibid., p. 186.

9 Ibid., p. 164–5.

10 Niccolò Machiavelli, *The Prince* [1532], trans. George Bull (Harmondsworth, 1961).

11 Plato, *The Republic*, trans. Francis MacDonald Cornford (Oxford, 1941), p. 75.

12 Ibid., p. 85.

13 Ibid.

14 Arthur Schopenhauer, *Essays and Aphorisms*, trans. R. J. Hollingdale (Harmondsworth, 1970), pp. 41, 43.

15 Ibid., p. 47.

16 Ibid., p. 54.

17 Ibid., p. 77.

18 Joshua Foa Dienstag, *Pessimism: Philosophy, Ethic, Spirit* (Princeton, NJ, 2006), p. 102.

19 Schopenhauer, *Essays and Aphorisms*, pp. 80, 81.

20 Arthur Schopenhauer, *The World as Will and Idea*, I–III, trans. R. B. Haldane and J. Kemp (London, 1906), I, p. 3.

21 Ibid., I, pp. 4–5.

22 Ibid., I, p. 213.

23 Ibid., I, p. 214.

24 Ibid., I, pp. 214–5.

25 Ibid., III, p. 392.

26 Ibid., II, p. 411.

27 Ibid., III, p. 383.

28 Introduction to Schopenhauer, *Essays and Aphorisms*, p. 22.

29 Friedrich Nietzsche, *Thus Spoke Zarathustra: A Book for Everyone and Nobody*, trans. Graham Parkes (Oxford, 2005), p. 11.

30 Ibid.

31 Friedrich Nietzsche, *On the Genealogy of Morals: A Polemic* [1887], trans. Douglas Smith (Oxford and New York, 1996), p. 7.

32 Ibid., p. 19.

33 Friedrich Nietzsche, 'On Truth and Lying in a Non–moral Sense' [1873], in *The Birth of Tragedy and Other Writings*, trans. Ronald Speirs, ed. Raymond Geuss and Ronald Speirs (Cambridge, 1999), p. 139–53 (p. 146).

34 Theodor W. Adorno and Max Horkheimer, *Dialectic of Enlightenment* [1944], trans. John Cumming (London, 1979), p. 3.

35 Theodor W. Adorno, *Negative Dialectics* [1966], trans. E. B. Ashton (London, 1973).

36 Jean-Paul Sartre, *Being and Nothingness: An Essay on Phenomenological Ontology* [1943], trans. Hazel E. Barnes (London, 1969), p. 471.

37 Ibid., p. 40.

38 Jean-Paul Sartre, *Nausea* [1938], trans. Robert Baldick (Harmondsworth, 1965), p. 15.

39 Ibid., pp. 32, 35.

40 Sartre, *Being and Nothingness*, p. 48.

41 Ibid., p. 59.

42 Ibid., p. 21.

43 Ibid., p. 115.

44 Albert Camus, *The Myth of Sisyphus* [1942], trans. Justin O'Brien (Harmondsworth, 1975), p. 11.

45 Ibid., pp. 110, 111.

46 Martin Heidegger, *Being and Time* [1927], trans. John MacQuarrie and Edward Robinson (Oxford, 1980), pp. 174.

47 Ibid., pp. 321, 329.

48 Ibid., p. 343.

49 Martin Heidegger, *Basic Writings: Martin Heidegger*, ed. David Farell Krell, 2nd edn (London and New York, 2011), p. 181.

50 Jacques Derrida, *Margins of Philosophy*, trans. Alan Bass (London, 1982), p. 3.

51 Jacques Derrida, *Writing and Difference*, trans. Alan Bass (Chicago, IL, 1978), p. 11.

52 Jacques Derrida, *Glas*, trans. J. P. Leavey and R. Rand (Lincoln, NA, and London, 1986).

53 Derrida, *Writing and Difference*, p. 292.

54 Stuart Sim, *Contemporary Continental Philosophy: The New Scepticism* (Aldershot and Burlington, VT, 2000), p. 2.

55 Jean-François Lyotard, *The Postmodern Condition: A Report on Knowledge*, trans. Geoff Bennington and Brian Massumi (Manchester, 1984), p. xxiv.

56 Ibid., p. 60.

57 John D. Barrow, *Impossibility: The Limits of Science and the Science of Limits* (London, 1998), p. 2.

58 Jean-François Lyotard, *Libidinal Economy*, trans. Iain Hamilton Grant (London, 1993), p. 96.

59 Jean-François Lyotard, *The Differend: Phrases in Dispute*, trans. Georges Van Den Abbeele (Manchester, 1988), p. xi.

60 Jean-François Lyotard, *The Inhuman: Reflections on Time*, trans. Geoffrey Bennington and Rachel Bowlby (Oxford, 1991), p. 2.

61 Michel Foucault, *Madness and Civilization: A History of Insanity in the Age of Reason*, trans. Richard Howard (London, 1971), p. 63.

62 Michel Foucault, *The History of Sexuality*, vol. I: *An Introduction*,
   trans. Robert Hurley (Harmondsworth, 1981), pp. 8–9.
   The other books making up the trilogy are, *The History of
   Sexuality*, vol. II: *The Use of Pleasure*, trans. Robert Hurley
   (Harmondsworth, 1987); and *The History of Sexuality*, vol. III:
   The Care of the Self, trans. Robert Hurley (Harmondsworth,
   1990).
63 Michel Foucault, *The Order of Things: An Archaeology of the
   Human Sciences* (New York, 1994), p. 387.
64 Richard Rorty, *Contingency, Irony, and Solidarity* (Cambridge,
   1989), p. 51.
65 Jean-François Lyotard, *Political Writings*, trans. Bill Readings
   and Kevin Paul Geiman (London, 1993), p. 64.
66 See, for example, Kurt Vonnegut, *Slaughterhouse-Five, or The
   Children's Crusade: A Duty-dance with Death* [1969] (London,
   1991), p. 5.
67 Roger Scruton, *The Uses of Pessimism and the Danger of False
   Hope* (Oxford, 2010), p. 5.

FIVE A World Without Meaning:
Pessimism in Literary Fiction

1 Sophocles, *Oedipus Rex*, in *The Theban Plays*, trans. E. F.
   Watling (Harmondsworth, 1947), p. 23.
2 J. R. Mulryne, Introduction to Thomas Kyd, *The Spanish
   Tragedy*, ed. J. R. Mulryne (London and Tonbridge, 1970),
   p. xxiii.
3 Christopher Marlowe, *The Jew of Malta*, in *The Complete
   Plays*, ed. J. B. Steane (Harmondsworth, 1969), Act II, scene iii,
   line 149, p. 377.
4 Introduction, ibid., pp. 28, 27.
5 Ibid., II.iii, l. 14, p. 383.
6 John Webster, *The Duchess of Malfi*, in *Three Plays*, ed. David
   Gunby (Harmondsworth, 1972), I.i, ll. 56–8, p. 177.
7 Ibid., I.i, l. 23, p. 175; I.i, l. 75, p. 177.
8 Cyril Tourneur, *The Revenger's Tragedy*, ed. Lawrence J. Ross
   (London, 1967), I.i, l. 95, p. 7.
9 Laurence Sterne, *The Life and Opinions of Tristram Shandy*,
   ed. Ian Campbell Ross (Oxford, 1983), p. 10.
10 Ibid., p. 5.

11 Ibid., p. 517.

12 Oliver Ready, Introduction to Fyodor Dostoevsky, *Crime and Punishment* [1866], trans. Oliver Ready (London, 2014), p. viii.

13 Fyodor Dostoevsky, *The Idiot*, trans. Alan Myers (Oxford, 1992), p. 14.

14 Quoted in Introduction, ibid., p. xv.

15 N. K. Mikhailovsky, quoted in Introduction to Fyodor Dostoevsky, *The Brothers Karamazov* [1880], trans. David McDuff (London, 2003), p. xxvi.

16 R. J. White, *Thomas Hardy and History* (London and Basingstoke, 1974), p. 16.

17 Thomas Hardy, *Tess of the D'Urbervilles: A Pure Woman* [1891], ed. P. N. Furbank (London and Basingstoke, 1974), p. 168.

18 Thomas Hardy, *Jude the Obscure* [1895], ed. P. N. Furbank (London and Basingstoke, 1974), p. 356.

19 Thomas Hardy, *Selected Shorter Poems of Thomas Hardy* (London and Basingstoke, 1975), p. 46.

20 Wilfred Owen, *The Poems of Wilfred Owen*, ed. Edmund Blunden (London, 1972), p. 55.

21 Siegfried Sassoon, 'Finished with the War: A Soldier's Declaration', in Robert Giddings, *The War Poets* (London, 1988), p. 111.

22 William Golding, *The Lord of the Flies* (London, 1958), p. 222.

23 Albert Camus, *The Plague*, trans. Stuart Gilbert (Harmondsworth, 1960), p. 252.

24 Ibid., p. 251.

25 Albert Camus, *The Outsider* [1947], trans. Stuart Gilbert (Harmondsworth, 1961), p. 48.

26 Ibid., p. 68.

27 Ibid., p. 81.

28 Ibid., p. 120.

29 Samuel Beckett, quoted in *Beckett at 60: A Festschrift*, ed. J. Calder (London, 1967), p. 34.

30 Samuel Beckett, *Company, Ill Seen Ill Said, Worstward Ho, Stirrings Still*, ed. Dirk Van Hulle (London, 2009), p. 81.

31 Samuel Beckett, *Waiting for Godot* [1953], in *The Complete Dramatic Works* (London and Boston, MA, 1986), p. 88.

32 Ibid., p. 83.

33 Samuel Beckett, *Breath* [1969], in *Complete Dramatic Works*, p. 371.

34 Samuel Beckett, *Krapp's Last Tape* [1958], in *Complete Dramatic Works*, p. 223.

35 Samuel Beckett, *Happy Days* [1961], in *Complete Dramatic Works*, p. 168.

36 James Ellroy, *LA Confidential* (London, 1994), p. 47.

37 James Lee Burke, *The Tin Roof Blowdown* (London, 2007), p. 2.

38 George Pelecanos, *Down by the River Where the Dead Men Go* (London, 1996), p. 221.

39 Ibid., p. 224.

40 Cormac McCarthy, *The Border Trilogy* (*All the Pretty Horses*; *The Crossing*; *Cities of the Plain*) (London, 2002), pp. 700–701.

41 Cormac McCarthy, *No Country for Old Men* (London, 2005), pp. 3–4.

42 Philip Roth, *The Plot Against America* (London, 2004), pp. 53–4.

43 Philip Roth, *Everyman* (London, 2007), pp. 91–2.

44 Philip Roth, *The Dying Animal* (London, 2006), p. 2.

six Visions of Despair: Pessimism in the Arts

1 Gwyn A. Williams, *Goya and the Impossible Revolution* (London, 1976), p. 1.

2 Antonina Vallentin, *This I Saw: The Life and Times of Goya*, trans. Katherine Woods (New York, 1949), p. 280.

3 Williams, *Goya and the Impossible Revolution*, p. 178.

4 Quoted in Iris Müller-Westermann, *Munch by Himself* (London, 2005), p. 43.

5 J. P. Hodin, *Edvard Munch* (London, 1972), p. 7.

6 Müller-Westermann, *Munch by Himself*, p. 43.

7 Quoted in Hodin, *Edvard Munch*, p. 76.

8 Quoted ibid., p. 60.

9 F. T. Marinetti, 'The Futurist Manifesto', in *Critical Writings*, trans. Doug Thompson, ed. Günther Berghaus (New York, 2006).

10 Timothy Hilton, *Picasso* (London, 1975), p. 246.

11 George Orwell, *Homage to Catalonia* [1938] (Harmondsworth, 1966), p. 240.

12 Ibid., p. 228.

13 Roland Penrose, *Miró* (London, 1970), p. 82.

14 Ibid., p. 84.

15 Ingmar Bergman, director, *The Seventh Seal*, in *Four Screenplays of Ingmar Bergman*, trans. Lars Malmstrom and David Kushner (New York, 1960), p. 112.

16 Ibid.

17 Ian MacDonald, *The New Shostakovich* (Oxford, 1991). A grisly fact to add in this context is that MacDonald later committed suicide.

18 Ibid., p. 7.

19 Quoted ibid., p. 6.

20 Sigmund Freud, *Standard Edition of the Complete Psychological Works of Sigmund Freud*, vol. III, trans. and ed. James Strachey (London, 1962), p. 170.

21 Although the original writer of the song is unknown, it was eventually claimed by Joe Primrose (a pseudonym for the jazz promoter and musician Irving Mills), but not until 1929, the year after Armstrong's famous recording. African American cynicism and pessimism about whites would hardly be lessened by such events.

SEVEN The Benefits of a Half-empty Glass: Pessimism as a Lifestyle

1 Arthur Schopenhauer, *The World as Will and Idea*, I–III, trans. R. B. Haldane and J. Kemp (London, 1906), III, pp. 460, 392.

2 More can be found in Joshua Foa Deinstag, *Pessimism: Philosophy, Ethic, Spirit* (Princeton, NJ, 2006)

BIBLIOGRAPHY

Adorno, Theodor W., *Prisms*, trans. Samuel and Shierry Weber
    (Cambridge, MA, 1981)
—, and Max Horkheimer, *Dialectic of Enlightenment* [1944], trans.
    John Cumming (London, 1979)
Barrow, John D., *Impossibility: The Limits of Science and the Science
    of Limits* (London, 1998)
Barthes, Roland, *Image Music Text*, trans. Stephen Heath (London,
    1977)
Bauman, Zygmunt, *Intimations of Postmodernity* (London, 1992)
Beckett, Samuel, *The Complete Dramatic Works* (London and
    Boston, MA, 1986)
—, *Company, Ill Seen Ill Said, Worstward Ho, Stirrings Still*,
    ed. Dirk Van Hulle (London, 2009)
Bergman, Ingmar, *Four Screenplays of Ingmar Bergman*, trans. Lars
    Malmstrom and David Kushner (New York, 1960)
Bulletin of the Atomic Scientists, LXX/3 (May 2014)
Bunyan, John, *Grace Abounding to the Chief of Sinners* [1666],
    ed. W. R. Owens (Harmondsworth, 1987)
—, *The Life and Death of Mr Badman* [1680], ed. James F. Forrest
    and Roger Sharrock (Oxford, 1988)
—, *The Pilgrim's Progress* [1678], ed. W. R. Owens (Oxford, 2003)
Burke, James Lee, *The Tin Roof Blowdown* (London, 2007)
Burney, Francis, *Cecilia* [1782], ed. Margaret Anne Doody and
    Peter Sabor (Oxford, 1988)
Burton, Robert, *The Anatomy of Melancholy* [1621], ed. Holbrook
    Jackson (London, 1932)
Calder, J., ed., *Beckett at 60: A Festschrift* (London, 1967)
Calvin, John, *Institutes of the Christian Religion* [1536], I–II, trans.

Ford Lewis Battles (London, 1961)

Camus, Albert, *The Plague* [1947], trans. Stuart Gilbert
(Harmondsworth, 1960)

—, *The Outsider* [1942], trans. Stuart Gilbert (Harmondsworth,
1961)

—, *The Myth of Sisyphus* [1942], trans. Justin O'Brien
(Harmondsworth, 1975)

Cixous, Hélène, 'The Laugh of the Medusa', in *New French
Feminisms*, ed. Elaine Marks and Isabelle de Courtivron
(Brighton, 1981), pp. 245–64

Cowling, Mark, 'Can Marxism Make Sense of Crime?', in *The
Legacy of Marxism: Contemporary Challenges, Conflicts and
Developments*, ed. Matthew Johnson (London and New York,
2012), pp. 135–47

Defoe, Daniel, *A Journal of the Plague Year* [1722], ed. Louis Landa
(London, 1969)

—, *Roxana: The Fortunate Mistress* [1724], ed. John Mullan
(Oxford, 1996)

—, *The Life and Strange Surprising Adventures of Robinson Crusoe*
[1719], ed. Thomas Keymer (London, 2007)

Derrida, Jacques, *Writing and Difference*, trans. Alan Bass
(Chicago, IL, 1978)

—, *Margins of Philosophy*, trans. Alan Bass (London, 1982)

Descartes, René, *Philosophical Writings*, trans. and ed. Elizabeth
Anscombe and Peter Thomas Geach (London, 1970)

Dickens, Charles, *Hard Times: For These Times* [1854], ed. David
Craig (Harmondsworth, 1969)

Dienstag, Joshua Foa, *Pessimism: Philosophy, Ethic, Spirit*
(Princeton, NJ, 2006)

Dostoevsky, Fyodor, *Crime and Punishment* [1866], trans. Oliver
Ready (London, 2014)

Ellroy, James, *The Big Nowhere* (London, 1990)

—, *The Black Dahlia* (London, 1993)

—, *White Jazz* (London, 1993)

—, *LA Confidential* (London, 1994)

Eysenck, Hans J., *Race, Intelligence and Education* (London, 1971)

Fielding, Henry, *Miscellanies*, in *The Wesleyan Edition of the Works
of Henry Fielding*, ed. Henry Knight Miller, I–III (Oxford, 1972)

Foucault, Michel, *Madness and Civilization: A History of Insanity
in the Age of Reason*, trans. Richard Howard (London, 1971)

—, *The History of Sexuality,* vol. I: *An Introduction,* trans. Robert Hurley (Harmondsworth, 1981); *The History of Sexuality,* vol. II: *The Use of Pleasure,* trans. Robert Hurley (Harmondsworth, 1987); *The History of Sexuality,* vol. III: *The Care of the Self,* trans. Robert Hurley (Harmondsworth, 1990)

—, *The Order of Things: An Archaeology of the Human Sciences* [1966] (New York, 1994)

Freud, Sigmund, *Standard Edition of the Complete Psychological Works of Sigmund Freud,* vol. III, trans. and ed. James Strachey (London, 1962)

Friedman, Milton, *Capitalism and Freedom,* 2nd edn [1962] (Chicago, IL, and London, 1982)

Gardner, Helen, ed., *The Metaphysical Poets* (Harmondsworth, 1966)

Gaskell, Elizabeth, *Mary Barton: A Tale of Manchester Life* [1848], ed. Stephen Gill (Harmondsworth, 1970)

Golding, William, *Lord of the Flies* (London, 1958)

Grossman, Lisa, 'Quantum Twist Could Kill Off the Multiverse', *New Scientist,* 14 May 2014, pp. 8–9

Hardy, Thomas, *Jude the Obscure* [1895], ed. P. N. Furbank (London and Basingstoke, 1974)

—, *Tess of the D'Urbervilles: A Pure Woman* [1891], ed. P. N. Furbank (London and Basingstoke, 1974)

—, *Selected Shorter Poems of Thomas Hardy* (London and Basingstoke, 1975)

Heidegger, Martin, *Being and Time* [1927], trans. John MacQuarrie and Edward Robinson (Oxford, 1980)

—, *Basic Writings: Martin Heidegger,* ed. David Farell Krell, 2nd edn (London and New York, 2011)

Hetschko, Clemens, Andreas Knabe, and Ronnie Schöb, 'Changing Identity: Retiring From Unemployment', *Economic Journal,* CXXIV/575 (2014), pp. 149–66

Hilton, Timothy, *Picasso* (London, 1975)

Hobbes, Thomas, *Leviathan, or, The Matter, Forme, and Power of a Free Common-wealth Ecclesiasticall and Civill* [1651], ed. C. B. Macpherson (Harmondsworth, 1968)

Hodin, J. P., *Edvard Munch* (London, 1972)

Hogg, James, *The Private Memoirs and Confessions of a Justified Sinner* [1824], ed. John Carey (Oxford, 1981)

Hume, David, *Enquiries Concerning Human Understanding and Concerning the Principles of Morals* [1748], 3rd edn, ed. P. H. Nidditch (Oxford, 1975)

Ingram, Allan, 'Deciphering Difference: A Study in Medical Literacy', in *Melancholy Experience in the Literature of the Long Eighteenth Century*, ed. Allan Ingram et al. (Basingstoke, 2011), pp. 170–202

Irigaray, Luce, *This Sex Which Is Not One*, trans. Catherine Porter, with Carolyn Burke (Ithaca, NY, 1985)

—, *Je, Tu, Nous: Towards a Culture of Sexual Difference*, trans. Alison Martin (New York and London, 1993)

The Koran, trans. N. J. Dawood (Harmondsworth, 1974)

Lawlor, Clark, 'Fashionable Melancholy', in *Melancholy Experience in the Literature of the Long Eighteenth Century*, ed. Allan Ingram et al. (Basingstoke, 2011), pp. 25–53

Leibniz, G. W., T*he Monadology and Other Philosophical Writings*, trans. Robert Latta (London, 1971)

Lewis, Michael, *Flash Boys: Cracking the Money Code* (London, 2014)

Lovelock, James, *The Revenge of Gaia: Earth's Climate Crisis and the Fate of Humanity* (London, 2006)

Lyotard, Jean-François, *The Postmodern Condition: A Report on Knowledge*, trans. Geoff Bennington and Brian Massumi (Manchester, 1984)

—, *The Differend: Phrases in Dispute*, trans. Georges Van Den Abbeele (Manchester, 1988)

—, *Libidinal Economy*, trans. Iain Hamilton Grant (London, 1993)

—, *Political Writings*, trans. Bill Readings and Kevin Paul Geiman (London, 1993)

McCarthy, Cormac, *The Border Trilogy* (*All the Pretty Horses*; *The Crossing*; *Cities of the Plain*) (London, 2002)

—, *No Country for Old Men* (London, 2005)

MacDonald, Ian, *The New Shostakovich* (Oxford, 1991)

Mankell, Henning, *The Troubled Man*, trans. Laurie Thompson (London, 2011)

Mantel, Hilary, *Eight Months on Ghazzah Street* [1988] (London, 2013)

Marinetti, F. T., *Critical Writings*, trans. Doug Thompson, ed. Günther Berghaus (New York, 2006)

Marlowe, Christopher, *The Complete Plays*, ed. J. B. Steane (Harmondsworth, 1969)

Marx, Karl, *Critique of the Gotha Programme* [1873], in Karl Marx
    and Frederick Engels, *Selected Works* (London, 1968)
Morris, Ian, *War! What Is It Good For? The Role of Conflict in
    Civilisation, from Primates to Robots* (London, 2014)
Müller-Westermann, Iris, *Munch by Himself* (London, 2005)
Nietzsche, Friedrich, *On the Genealogy of Morals: A Polemic*
    [1887], trans. Douglas Smith (Oxford and New York, 1996)
—, 'On Truth and Lying in a Non-Moral Sense' [1873], in *The
    Birth of Tragedy and Other Writings*, trans. Ronald Speirs,
    ed. Raymond Geuss and Ronald Speirs (Cambridge, 1999)
—, *Thus Spoke Zarathustra: A Book for Everyone and Nobody*
    [1883–5], trans. Graham Parkes (Oxford, 2005)
Orwell, George, *Homage to Catalonia* [1938] (Harmondsworth,
    1966)
Owen, Wilfred, *The Poems of Wilfred Owen*, ed. Edmund Blunden
    (London, 1972)
Pelecanos, George, *A Firing Offense* (London, 1992)
—, *Down by the River Where the Dead Men Go* (London, 1996)
—, *Nick's Trip* (London, 1998)
Penrose, Roland, *Miró* (London, 1970)
Piketty, Thomas, *Capital in the Twenty-first Century*, trans. Arthur
    Goldhammer (Cambridge, MA, 2014)
Plato, *The Republic*, trans. Francis MacDonald Cornford (Oxford,
    1941)
Ridley, Matt, *The Rational Optimist: How Prosperity Evolves*
    (London, 2010)
Rorty, Richard, *Contingency, Irony, and Solidarity* (Cambridge, 1989)
Roth, Philip, *The Plot Against America* (London, 2004)
—, *The Dying Animal* (London, 2006)
—, *Everyman* (London, 2007)
Sartre, Jean-Paul, *Nausea* [1938], trans. Robert Baldick
    (Harmondsworth, 1965)
—, *Being and Nothingness: An Essay on Phenomenological Ontology*
    [1943], trans. Hazel E. Barnes (London, 1969)
Sassoon, Siegfried, 'Finished with the War: A Soldier's Declaration',
    in *The War Poets*, ed. Robert Giddings (London, 1988)
Schopenhauer, Arthur, *The World as Will and Idea*, I–III,
    trans. R. B. Haldane and J. Kemp (London, 1906)
—, *Essays and Aphorisms*, trans. R. J. Hollingdale
    (Harmondsworth, 1970)

Scruton, Roger, *The Uses of Pessimism and the Danger of False Hope* (Oxford, 2010)

Sextus Empiricus, *Outlines of Scepticism*, trans. Julia Annas and Jonathan Barnes (Cambridge, 1994)

Shakespeare, William, *Hamlet*, ed. Harold Jenkins (London and New York, 1982)

Sim, Stuart, *Contemporary Continental Philosophy: The New Scepticism* (Aldershot and Burlington, VT, 2000)

Singh, Simon, *Big Bang: The Most Important Scientific Discovery of All Time and Why You Need to Know About It* (London and New York, 2004)

Sophocles, *The Theban Plays*, trans. E. F. Watling (Harmondsworth, 1947)

Standing, Guy, *The Precariat: The New Dangerous Class* (London, 2011)

—, *A Precariat Charter: From Denizens to Citizens* (London, 2014)

Sterne, Laurence, *The Life and Opinions of Tristram Shandy* [1759], ed. Ian Campbell Ross (Oxford, 1983)

Stoppard, Tom, *Jumpers* (London, 1986)

Tourneur, Cyril, *The Revenger's Tragedy*, ed. Lawrence J. Ross (London, 1967)

Webster, John, *Three Plays*, ed. David Gunby (Harmondsworth, 1972)

Williams, Gwyn A., *Goya and the Impossible Revolution* (London, 1976)

Wittig, Monique, *Les Guérillères*, trans. David Le Vay (New York, 1973)

ACKNOWLEDGEMENTS

Special thanks go to Ben Hayes at Reaktion for all his advice and support in the development of this project. As always, Dr Helen Brandon listened patiently to the arguments, read drafts and made helpful suggestions throughout the writing process.

INDEX

197